SERENITY
IMMORTALITY
HYPOTHESIS

SERENITY
IMMORTALITY
HYPOTHESIS

RONALD M CAPLAN MDCM FACS FACOG FRCSC

Copyrighted Material

Serenity Hypothesis
Copyright © 2024 RMC Publishing LLC
https://rmcpublishingllc.com

All rights reserved.
No part of this publication may be reproduced, stored in a retrieval system or transmitted, in any form or by any means—electronic, mechanical, photocopying, recording or otherwise—without prior written permission from the publisher, except for the inclusion of brief quotations in a review.

978-1-7350093-7-7 (paperback)
978-1-7350093-9-1 (hardcover)
978-1-7350093-8-4 (ebook)

Front Cover Art by Bill Rabinovitch: Serenity
Back Cover Art by Ellen Altfest: Green Spot
Back Cover Photo Credit: Daphne Youree
About the Author Photo Credit: Laurie Spens

DISCLAIMER

The contents of this book and e-book and all materials contained therein (collectively, the "Book") are provided for informational purposes only. The Book is not intended to be a substitute for professional medical advice, diagnosis, or treatment. The information provided in the Book should not be used by medical professionals for the purpose of diagnosing or treating a health condition or disease. You should always seek the advice of your physician or other qualified health provider if you have questions regarding a medical condition. Never disregard professional medical advice or delay in seeking it because of something you may have read in the Book. No physician-patient relationship is created by this Book. Neither the author nor the publisher makes any representation, express or implied, with respect to the information provided herein or to its use.

If you think you may have a medical emergency, call your doctor or 911 immediately. The author does not recommend or endorse any specific tests, physicians, products, procedures, opinions, or other information that may be mentioned in this Book. The Book is provided on an "as is" basis, and reliance on any information provided in this Book is solely at your own risk.

CONTENTS

Preface:	**Life Force**	**1**
Chapter 1:	**The Relationship of Consciousness and Serenity**	**7**
	What is Consciousness?	7
	Collective Consciousness	8
	Cosmic Consciousness	8
Chapter 2:	**Perception and Reality: The Limits of Sensation**	**13**
Chapter 3:	**Life and Death**	**17**
Chapter 4:	**Religion and Science**	**23**
Chapter 5:	**Psychoanalysis, Hypnosis, Regression Therapy, Persistence of Consciousness**	**29**
Chapter 6:	**Panpsychism**	**33**
Chapter 7:	**The Scientific Method, Rationalism, Empiricism**	**35**
Chapter 8:	**Theories**	**37**
	Model-Dependent Realism, M-Theory	37
	Big Bang Theory	38
	Quantum Theory	38
	Supersymmetry	40
	Grand Unified Theory (GUT) of Physics	40
	Theory of Everything (TOE)	40

Chapter 9:	**Theoretical Coalescence: The Serenity Hypothesis**	**45**
	Astronomical Observations	46
Chapter 10:	**Wilder Penfield MD: Getting the Picture Straight**	**49**
Chapter 11:	**Medicine: Science, Art, Calling**	**51**
Chapter 12:	**The Prolongation of Life and Consciousness; Aging and its Reversal**	**61**
Chapter 13:	**The Neurodegeneration Dilemma**	**71**
Chapter 14:	**Artificial Intelligence (AI)**	**75**
Chapter 15:	**Theories of Consciousness**	**81**
Chapter 16:	**Subjective Experience**	**85**

Serenity Hypothesis: References, Links — **89**

About the Author — **111**

SERENITY HYPOTHESIS | ART

Artist	Work	Location
Jean Paul Riopelle	Loin des Vitres	Following Preface
Bill Rabinovitch	Serenity	Following Chapter 1
Victor Salmones	The Search	Following Chapter 3
Jack Bush	Red on White Circle	Following Chapter 8
Ellen Altfest	Green Spot	Following Chapter 12
Kim Keever	Reverse Perspective	Following Chapter 14

PREFACE
LIFE FORCE

What is Life Force? What animates us, makes us appear bigger than we are, more than the sum of our physical parts?

Is it consciousness, awareness of self, place, time and purpose?

Does it arise from within, or penetrate from without?

Is it playing to other people, so that they see us as other than what we are, or as we really are?

Is it simply dynamism? Is it why we gravitate to leaders who exude confidence, even quiet confidence?

Is it evident in the ability to resist carping and negativity as we attempt to break through, to rise to the top, to be inventive, to create and explore?

Is it courage? The courage to trust one's own instincts over the admonishments of others?

Is it mutual reassurance, a reaction to vulnerability?

Is it tied to our ability to procreate, to live in, with and through another, and build a family, a community, a nation?

Can we bequeath it to machines with Artificial Intelligence? Do we want to?

Is it ours to bequeath? To bequeath only as a gift with our DNA?

Or a gift to keep?

Why are most people in our supposedly enlightened modern world believers in an external presence, in a soul?

Why do others mistrust our abilities, consider our survival an anathema, are imbued with self-doubt, even self-hate?

Is the Soul the Life Force? Are they synonymous? Do they exist?

Are we just giving names to things we don't understand, and that don't really exist as independent entities?

What did the Ancients know that we don't? Anything?

And what do we really know of what they knew, or thought? Fragments?

Were they just extrapolating from imperfect knowledge? Superstition?

Is the Scientific Method perfect? Valid?

Hypothesis? Theory? Fact?

How much of what we generally believe as fact is simply extrapolation from limited knowledge, or even pure conjecture?

If we can't prove existence of an entity, does that mean it doesn't exist?

What is thinking? Merely synapses firing? Something more?

Is there a Critical Mass that need to be surpassed?

What is Self-Fulfilling Prophecy? Does it work?

What do Physicians know that you don't? Physicists? Philosophers?

Why the yearning for a Unified Theory?

And what are We extrapolating from? We know our knowledge is imperfect, merely scratching the surface.

Why do we feel so protective of a sleeping child, the same child who exhausts us when awake?

Why do we only realize how fragile and small people were when we gaze upon their lifeless body after death?

And what is death, aside from the absence of life?

Why do we sleep? Why is sleep often troubled?

Why do we die?

And when does life cease?

How about near-death experience? The White Light?

Simply Anoxia?

Loin des Vitres | Jean Paul Riopelle

Jean Paul Riopelle (1923-2002) : Centenary
https://fondationriopelle.com/en/2023-the-centenary/

"Celebrating a Centenary of Artistic Genius"
https://fondationriopelle.com/en/artwork/

Loin des Vitres : English translation: (far) away from the windows: could Riopelle have been referring to our level of enlightenment?

https://www.youtube.com/watch?v=LnT66tlUrDw

…subtle inference of a large multidimensional circle: cosmologic?

…white and colored bits on a darker field… evokes quantum theory?

Loin des Vitres, 1968 © Estate of Jean Paul Riopelle / CARCC Ottawa 2024

CHAPTER 1
THE RELATIONSHIP OF CONSCIOUSNESS AND SERENITY

Serenity and peace[1,2,3] are at the highest levels that consciousness can achieve in many Eastern philosophies. In Western society we strive for peace on both a physical (absence of conflict and war) and emotional (absence of psychic turmoil) level, and the consequent serenity it brings. Our highest level spiritual and philosophical thinkers often notably present a serene appearance and seem to be at peace with themselves, as do many older people in their later years. An innate understanding of our place in the cosmos could confer an anxiety-alleviating serenity.

What is Consciousness? Simply and broadly put, consciousness is awareness[4,5,6]. It is impossible to argue for or against the presence of consciousness in a given circumstance without agreement as to what consciousness is, and how it manifests its presence. Chalmers has pointed out the "hard problem" of understanding consciousness[198,205].

Hippocrates identified the brain as the interpreter of consciousness.[7]

Significant ongoing research at an accelerating pace might eventually lead to further clarification of the conscious state. The research starts from different directions. The Human Connectome Project[95] is an example of starting from the microscopic anatomical level, looking at the connections between brain cells. The US National Institutes of Health's Brain Research through Advancing Innovative Neurotechnologies Initiative-Cell Census Network (BICCN) has discovered previously unknown types of brain cells.[208]

The other direction involves studying people with Alzheimer's Disease, other forms of dementia, and levels of loss of consciousness, and seeing how they differ from healthy individuals, including differences on a submicroscopic level.

When someone is unconscious there is a lack of awareness, among other things, of their surroundings (where they are in place and time) and their personal status, condition and needs.

Coma[8] is deep, unarousable unconsciousness. The affected person does not react to painful stimuli.

Collective consciousness[9] most usually is taken to mean social norms: shared ideas, beliefs, attitudes, and knowledge that operate as a unifying force in a society. On another level, the philosopher William James[10,11,12] considered cosmic consciousness to be a collective consciousness.

Cosmic Consciousness [13], a concept used by the philosopher Edward Carpenter[14], was elucidated by the Canadian psychiatrist Maurice Bucke in 1901, a year before he died (at just about the same age I am now) in his book, Cosmic Consciousness: A Study in the Evolution of the Human Mind. Bucke wrote that we are "specks of relative death in an infinite ocean of life"[15]. Bucke, a friend of the poet Walt Whitman, inferred that he had an epiphany and experienced cosmic consciousness after reading Leaves of Grass[170]. Bucke and I both attended McGill University Medical School with a gap of a hundred years or so.

The psychologist and philosopher William James wrote a year later in The Varieties of Religious Experience (1902) that what we experience in our ordinary lives "is but one special type of consciousness."[12] James considered cosmic consciousness to be a collective consciousness which manifests itself in the mind and remains intact after death, possibly retaining traces of the life history of the individual emanation. Cosmic consciousness can be described as transcendence, or a flash of intellectual illumination. James was a president of the Society for Psychical Research, organized to investigate paranormal phenomena.

Long before, the Enlightenment metaphysical[195] philosopher[193] Immanuel Kant[194] wrote about "the existence and personality of the same rational being continuing endlessly."[192]

Metaphysics is a branch of philosophy that deals with matters including being and knowing.[193.] Alan Lightman, in his book The Transcendent Brain, tells how The Enlightenment scholar Moses Mendelssohn went a step further, postulating the perfection of the "universal soul."[189, 190] Mendelssohn himself in 1767 created a German version with changes of Plato's Phaedo[191], known as the Phaedon[190], which discusses The Death of Socrates and the Immortality of the Soul.[190]

In Transcendental Meditation, Cosmic Consciousness is the fifth highest level (out of seven) of consciousness.

Serenity | Bill Rabinovitch

> **"I am constantly trying to evolve my work and push my boundaries. My art making reflects a process of spontaneous invention and poetic feeling—while exploring the potentials of great color."**

Bill Rabinovitch has been part of the SoHo Art world for 50 years. He is a painter of great originality who created historic art events such as his Whitney Counterweight throughout SoHo during the Whitney Museum's Biennial. He was a jet pilot in the USAF & project planner for NASA. His decade long, award-winning Artseen tv cable series including his plays and documentaries about Picasso, Basquiat, Schnabel & James Rosenquist, now on YouTube, are part of art world lore. He has explored a new **Digital advanced consciousness**. He knew Andy Warhol and did the large painting honoring him, now entitled **"Serenity"** reproduced here that Andy very much admired. A documentary about Bill's life was produced & shown by WPIX Ch 11 in 2023.

Serenity, Bill Rabinovitch (born 1936)
https://www.billrabinovitch.com/about

CHAPTER 2

PERCEPTION AND REALITY: THE LIMITS OF SENSATION

We live in a narrow bandwidth of the reality that surrounds us. Our vision is restricted to light between ultraviolet and infrared. Its keenness pales by comparison to that of an eagle. Our sense of smell is vastly inferior to our dogs'. That is one good reason for our affection for dogs over millennia: dogs increase our perception and warn us of predators, and often can ward them off. Another reason, of course, is their unstinting loyalty and affection. Our hearing is confined to the sound frequency range 20 Hz to 20kHz.[17] Sophisticated instrumentation, investigation and exploration have widened our grasp of the true nature of the environment and universe we live in, as well as making us aware of how little of the enormity and complexity of it we know or understand, both on a macroscopic and submicroscopic level.

Bending of the time-space continuum[18], multiple dimensions[19] and string theory[20,21] are all considered plausible.

Rene Descartes famously answered the question of the reality of our existence by stating Cogito Ergo Sum: I think, therefore I am[22]. However, we now know that the universe we perceive in our daily existence via our senses is only a small piece of what is out, and in, there.

Albert Einstein, with his Theory of Special Relativity[233], began to alter our perception of reality more than a hundred years ago, in 1905. Small amounts of mass (m) can become large amounts of energy (E): $E=mc^2$.

"c" is the speed of light.

Ten years later, he elucidated his Theory of General Relativity[234], by which gravity is considered to arise from the curvature of space-time, which by itself is a perception altering concept.

Einstein [23]was familiar with the writings of Bucke.[24]

Evidence of an expanding universe[25], leading to the theory that our universe had a beginning (Genesis:[26] In the beginning…) caused some to reconsider the existence of a prime mover, or deity.

Chateau Frontenac[27] Plains of Abraham, Quebec City circa late 1960's: Male figure silently present at end of long hallway, 17th Century garb: rose colored coat, britches, powdered wig. Matter-of-fact couple: I, a surgeon, she, an entrepreneur, exiting our room for dinner: both see him and are bemused.

Inquiry at desk: Desk clerk stoic. No employees or guests in such garb, not a holiday. No parties on schedule. The couple proceed to dinner, unaware that other reports existed.

Being busy with "practical" matters, including a full surgical schedule and raising a family, I never really thought about this episode (except occasionally as amusing cocktail party chatter) until recently, some fifty years later. Very superficial online investigation revealed that there have been numerous similar reports, some much more embellished. I now understand why the desk clerk was so closemouthed.

Is Inspiration the distillation of a multitude of thought processes over time into a single conclusion: the AHA! Moment, or is it this plus something else? For some months I have been thinking about coalescing the knowledge I have gained in a lifetime of observing and treating patients and studying the human condition and the diseases that afflict us, in a medical- philosophical treatise, but didn't have the impetus or energy to do so. Then one morning the focus of this treatise and its title came to me within minutes and I began to write. Coincidence? Or something else….

CHAPTER 3
LIFE AND DEATH

These are defined terms. The definitions of those words, and usage are becoming increasingly constrained as our knowledge increases, at present logarithmically. In humans, life is no longer considered to occur at the moment of birth, and in prenatal terms the debated issue has largely gone over to the onset of awareness (consciousness?) for medicolegal purposes.

What defines life has changed from a discussion of entropy[28], the measurement of disorder or randomness in a system, and the ability to deal with it, which machines are now capable of doing.

Life[29] is the capacity to metabolize, grow, reproduce, function and change (adapt). The classic vital functions to assess continuing life are brain activity, respiration and cardiac activity. Adequacy of urine output can be assessed, as can liver function. The vital organs without which life cannot be sustained are the brain, heart, lungs, liver and kidneys.

In medical usage, the definition of the cessation of life has gone from absence of breathing and pulse, to absence of breathing, heart rate and pulse with dilated fixed pupils, to flatlining with a demonstrable absence of cardiac activity, to cessation of demonstrable brain function, with no electroencephalographic activity. Cessation of activity by vital organs has also been cited (lungs, heart, liver, kidneys, brain). We know that not all body cells are necessarily dead (ceased functioning, loss of metabolic activity) at that point. Vital organ transplantation (first kidney, then heart, lung, liver) is now considered quite commonplace.

Triage decisions are focused mainly on who can be brought back via cardiopulmonary resuscitation, and with what degree of permanent incapacity, taking into consideration the presence or absence of widespread (presently) incurable disease. These decisions are made in the context of society: how advanced the society is, how stable, war or peacetime, frontline or rearguard, pandemic or not, level and proximity of medical facilities/services, religious and societal beliefs and practices, individual's stated or written wishes.

Defining death[30,31], and the moment of death, relies on the definition of life. The most facile definition of death is the absence of life in an entity that previously had life; that is, the cessation of life.

Death (defined term) is the cessation of Life (defined term). The exact Time of Death is the time a physician enters on a Death Certificate. On that basis, it is certainly possible that some vestige of consciousness as we know it might, and probably does, on occasion survive the official time of death.

It follows that Afterlife is a term whose definition relies on the chosen definition of life.

Immortality infers eternal life, and the absence of death. Life, among other things, is the absence of death; immortality is the absence of death forever.

Near Death Experience describes sensations felt by an individual in cardiac arrhythmia or arrest, who is anoxic, and unconscious to the outside observer, or semi-conscious. The scientific explanation might invoke hallucinations secondary to cerebral anoxia, hypercarbia (abnormally increased Carbon Dioxide in the blood), abnormal activity in the temporal lobe of the brain, or actual brain damage.

Sensations of feeling outside one's body and looking down on it from above have similarly been evoked during brain surgery with stimulation of the temporal lobe of the brain (Penfield). Borjigin noted increased gamma electrical activity in the temporo-parieto-occipital junction of the brain, an area involved in consciousness that is active during dreaming, seizures, and out-of-body experiences. Borjigin believes that the burst of brain activity after cessation of heartbeat is part of a survival mode that the brain enters when deprived of oxygen. The brain releases signaling molecules and creates abnormal brainwave patterns, possibly in an attempt to resuscitate itself, while shutting down external signs of consciousness.[188]

The Search | Victor Salmones

Realist nude sculpture
http://victorsalmones.com/hist.html

What is the meaning of the two identical faces (mask?) at arm's length?

Entanglement?

Searching for identity?

Salmones, Victor (1937-1989): *The Search*. 1981, bronze
Photograph Courtesy of Sotheby's

CHAPTER 4
RELIGION AND SCIENCE

The fact that the vast majority of humanity has, and has had, religious faith through the millennia[32] is not scientific proof that there is a deity, or that consciousness, or a soul exists beyond life. Zen koans can be taken to mean that proof is not necessarily needed[182]. The vast majority of people used to believe that the earth is flat, and that the sun revolves around us. That turned out to be erroneous. On the other hand, scientific theories are often debunked as well, which is an accepted part of science.

It is WHY the vast majority of humanity holds these beliefs that constitutes some proof. All the myriad manifestations that are attributed to the presence of some prime mover cannot easily be written off by Darwinism[33] (random selection and survival of the fittest), as an arbitrary convention, figure of speech, as the mistaken interpretations of disordered, or superstitious, naïve, uneducated minds, as improper application of the Scientific Method, as a simple lack of oxygen to the brain (anoxia), or physical damage to the brain itself (epileptogenic focus, stroke).

Scientists are delving deeper past the microscopic to the submicroscopic level, while at the same time going from basic biologic building blocks to assembling more and more complex forms, and using recently discovered techniques of genetic manipulation, cutting strands of DNA[34,35], rearranging DNA molecules to create recombinant DNA molecules constructed from segments obtained from different DNA molecules.[36,37,38,39]

Physicians are probing the human body with increasingly sophisticated techniques including ultrasonography, imaging by reflecting high energy 'sound' waves off objects. The waves have higher frequency than sound that can be heard by humans. Four dimensional ultrasonography is real time ultrasonography, time being the fourth dimension. For example, a fetus can be visualized within its mother's womb (uterus), moving its limbs and body as these movements actually occur. The conventional three dimensions are, of course, length, height, and width.

When doing sonography, blood vessels can be imaged in color, and the blood flow through those vessels seen and measured. This is known as color flow doppler. One use of this is the visualization of the umbilical cord of the growing fetus in the uterus. The quality of blood flow through the umbilical vessels is an indicator of fetal wellbeing.

The Doppler Effect refers to the difference in sound as it moves away from you. The classic example is the variance in sound of a train whistle, as the train passes you.

Magnetic Resonance Imaging (MRI)[40] is an advanced imaging technique that uses a powerful magnet to alter polarity.

Three and four dimensional CAT[41] scans (Computerized axial tomography) are widely used today. The fourth dimension is time. CAT stands for computerized axial tomography, an advanced, computerized imaging technique that very quickly takes serial Xrays through the body in thin 'slices', so that very small abnormalities can be found.

Spiral CT scan is fast and painless. The technique can be used to detect very early masses, or lesions, in the chest, for the early diagnosis of lung cancer. The technique is also used to detect calcifications in the coronary arteries supplying blood to the heart. Significant coronary artery disease can be detected while the person being studied is still entirely symptom free, and before any heart attack occurs.

PET[42] (Positron emission tomography) scans utilize glucose tagged with a radioactive isotope to gauge its metabolism. The person being imaged is given sugar, which is tagged by a radioactive isotope. Malignant cells tend to metabolize sugar at a higher rate, because they are actively growing and dividing. The increased radioactive uptake measured at a given site in the body infers that there may be a malignant tumor at that site.

Angiography is a technique utilizing dye which can be seen on imaging. The dye is injected into blood vessels to see if they are being obstructed by atherosclerotic plaque formation. The technique is used, for example, in the carotid arteries in the neck, which supply blood to the brain, and in blood vessels leading to the coronary arteries, which supply blood to the heart.

Bronchoscopy is used to observe and gather tissue and fluid from the passages to the lungs.

Mediastinoscopy is a step further in which a scope is introduced into the mediastinum, the space around the great blood vessels and the heart, usually in cases of cancer requiring staging and grading prior to definitive therapy.

Colonoscopy is now widely, and correctly, publicized for its role in the early detection of bowel cancer and precancerous growths in the large intestine. The scope can be passed through the entire large intestine. The physician watches the entire examination on a television monitor and takes biopsies of suspicious areas.

Upper GI (gastrointestinal) monitoring may be carried out with an endoscope passed into the esophagus.

New intricate complexities are found which remain to be elucidated. The deeper we probe, the more wonders unfold. Scientists encounter biologic fail-safe mechanisms[171,172] and system redundancies that go far beyond having paired vital organs (eg kidneys). We now know of receptor[43] sites on cells and how they function. Receptor sites are distinctively shaped areas on cell surfaces, designed to receive specific substances.

There are telomeres[44,45,46] on the ends of DNA with enzymatic[47] control by telomerase[48]. We are aware of programmed cell death[49].

It is not surprising that so many scientists, physicians, and physician-scientists believe in a higher order. Some years ago it was thought that "intelligent, rational" people would follow logic and the scientific method to debunk such belief systems, as we discovered the basic truths of life on a microscopic scale and explored the cosmos. We now realize that the more we learn, the more exquisite complexity is revealed.

I visited the then Soviet Union during the beginnings of Glasnost[50]. I was solemnly assured while visiting an Orthodox church that religion was superstition practiced by unenlightened and poorly educated inferior non-Communists, for whom one should feel sorry (in between bouts of persecution). I have heard some of those same mutterings in our own society, and still hear them currently.

When asked in my professional capacity why so many bad things happen in the world, and specifically to unsuspecting individual people, I would suggest when appropriate that the affiliated religious authority be consulted. It is much more satisfying in medicine to have a clearcut etiology (cause) for a condition, a proven treatment, and a clear path to recovery than having to attribute a medical event to "God's Will." Fortunately, our ability to prevent, or diagnose potentially life-threatening conditions at a very early stage is increasing rapidly. Similarly, our ability to effectively treat, often in a targeted way, and manage such conditions is improving greatly.

In casual conversation my answer to that same "why" question tends to be "God is busy". This reflects the attitude of many scientists, including the late Carl Sagan[51,52], who recognized the vast complexity of the cosmos. Sagan was intrigued by the possibility of extraterrestrial life.[210]

In response to a child's question concerning who or what is God, my answer is "God is a concept." I have yet to be asked the follow-up question "What is a concept?"

CHAPTER 5
PSYCHOANALYSIS, HYPNOSIS, REGRESSION THERAPY, PERSISTENCE OF CONSCIOUSNESS

My colleague, and one of my best friends in life, was the brilliant, incredibly brave, accomplished published psychiatrist, the late Dr. Sidney Lecker, who early on espoused Biofeedback[53] as a method of stress control.

Throughout my life, I personally did not have need for this type of intervention. I discovered that while an undergraduate student in psychology. I was in a soundproof room with earphones on solving increasingly difficult problems while the investigator was trying to harass me via the earphones in order to assess the effects on my efficiency and accuracy at the task. The more he tried, the more serene I became, and went with the flow of my consciousness towards solving the problems. He finally remotely administered an electric shock. At that point, I took off the monitoring devices and earphones and went outside to seek out the experimenter. Luckily for at least one of us, I did not find him.

For the majority of my professional life, I was available to my patients at all hours of every day. I learned to sleep when I could, almost by self-hypnosis [54]. I could consciously "let go" mentally into a serene state. I have subsequently tried on occasion to see if I could identify the exact moment in time when wakefulness turns into sleep: I never could. This could be considered analogous to the blurry line of life morphing into death.

I enjoyed my many hours as a surgeon in the operating room. The more complex the task, the more engrossed, focused and calm I became, to the exclusion of outside stimuli. Something similar happens to me when I write, but not with the same level of intensity. I lose track of time.

Sid and I interned together. More than fifty years ago, as a team we tried to resuscitate a patient who had gone into cardiac arrest by using the then fledgling, low percentage success technique of CPR (cardiopulmonary resuscitation), to no avail. We pronounced him dead: that is, as physicians we defined the moment of death in keeping with the objective criteria for that diagnosis in use at that time.[30,31]

Sid was intrigued by neuroscience and the linked pioneering studies in experimental psychology then being led by the groundbreaking Dr Donald Hebb[55], who I studied under in my premedical years. The approach of linking physical science and psychology had previously been undertaken in the collaboration of Carl Jung and the Nobel Prize winning physicist Wolfgang Pauli.[231]

Sid went on to gain certification in psychiatry, and in order as well to be certified as a psychoanalyst, underwent psychoanalysis,[56] during which he was schooled in regression therapy[57] and the tools of hypnosis.[58] In a matter-of-fact manner he told me that he could remember a traumatic event from his infancy.

At a young age, Dr Lecker became Assistant Commissioner for Psychiatric Affairs for the State of New York, and although the Three Mile Island nuclear disaster [59] in 1979 occurred in Pennsylvania, he was one of the first investigating and treating psychiatrists on the scene. He died in 1986 after visibly suffering for years, without complaint, with a very virulent cancer, quite uncommon in young men, at age forty-nine. The report of the commission that investigated Three Mile Island stated there was no statistical increase in fatal cancer incidence among the survivors. Because Dr Lecker was not working or living there at the exact time of the occurrence, he was not counted. We now know the toll taken on first responders in disasters, brutally brought home to us in the Twin Towers attack in New York City. We also know that conclusions reached by commissions, even assuming impartiality, can at best be only as good as the completeness of the data that is considered.

I gave Sid's eulogy. I remember clearly stating that he was immortal, at the very least via the DNA he had passed on to his remarkable children.

Regression therapy has been taken further, with people stating that they remember past lives. Major Eastern religions including Hinduism, and Buddhism whose believers aspire to Nirvana³ with no further rebirths, espouse reincarnation. Inner peace is frequently cited as a higher ideal in major religions. There is the aspiration to ascend at death to a higher, or better level.

CHAPTER 6
PANPSYCHISM

Does the cosmos itself have a form of consciousness? In 2016, the physicist Gregory Matloff[60] proposed a universal proto-consciousness[61] (primordial consciousness) field in the Journal of Consciousness Exploration and Research. This is a mind-bending concept. It is backed by the Integrated Information Theory elucidated by Kleiner and Tull[62,63] previously enunciated by Guilio Tononi in 2004.[64] I have sometimes looked at such theories the way the ancient Greeks must have considered the fifth century BC atomic theory proposed by Democritus: not provable, of no practical consequence, and just one of many theories about the nature of matter. Aristotle[65] whose thinking about the conscious mind is notable, effectively debunked the atomic theory for his contemporaries and for some time afterwards because of his intellectual stature. The fact that the atomic theory[66] was correct made no difference then, and for at least 2300 years thereafter, when John Dalton[67] scientifically tested the theory. He was followed by such luminaries as Rutherford,[68] Bohr[69], Einstein[23] and Oppenheimer[70] and the team who finally brought the stark reality of atomic theory home to the world's population in a blinding flash of light.

Looking at panpsychism from another perspective, the concept of a universal protoconsciousness comes close to being a religious concept, as does the concept of cosmic consciousness, especially until conclusive proof can be given. It should be remembered that religious leaders are comfortable with the proofs of their faiths, irrespective of the fact that they do not meet current scientific standards. The recording of a personal encounter or experience two or five thousand years ago could be considered to be just as valid as a contemporary encounter.

CHAPTER 7
THE SCIENTIFIC METHOD, RATIONALISM, EMPIRICISM

First elucidated in the 17th century, the Scientific Method[71] involves systematic observation, measurement, experimentation and testing, inductive (theory development) and deductive (testing theory) reasoning[72], leading to modification of hypotheses (proposed explanations; predictions) and theories (substantial explanations of occurrences).[73]

Rationalism[74] involves the accumulation of knowledge independent of sensory experience. Rational thinking involves accessing, organizing, and analyzing information and considering the variables.

Empiricism[75] values sense experience as the source of knowledge. Evolving Artificial Intelligence (AI) utilizes both approaches.

CHAPTER 8
THEORIES

Model-Dependent Realism, M-Theory

Model-Dependent Realism[76] is the approach taken by Hawking and Mlodinow in the Mystery of Being, in their book The Grand Design. The brain conceptualizes the world from the elements of sensory input, forming theories that can explain events. The physical theory or world picture is a mathematical "model and a set of rules that connect the elements of the model to observations."[78] Hawking and Mlodinow are up to M-Theory[77] (Witten[169]) as a candidate for the ultimate theory of everything.

M-theory is a family of overlapping theories that attempt to answer why there is something rather than nothing, and why we exist. Among other things, M-theory predicts that our universe, which is not the only universe, may have been created out of nothing.[76]

In the recent book On the Origin of Time: Stephen Hawking's Final Theory by Thomas Hertog [178], reviewed by Robert P. Crease[179], the Final Theory of the Universe is that it is 'holographic'; a four-dimensional membrane in a five-dimensional space, a small part of a larger reality. The fourth dimension is Space-Time[181]. The fifth dimension, according to Oskar Klein, is a dimension in which gravity and electromagnetism unite to create a theory of the fundamental forces.[180]

Cosmologists observe the universe from an exterior perspective. But quantum mechanics, in which the act of observing creates what is observed, make cosmologists the fixers of cosmic origins. "It is," Hertog writes, "as if the act of observation today retroactively fixes the outcome of the big bang."[179]

Big Bang Theory[78,79] posits that our universe had a finite beginning, at the beginning of time: almost 14 billion years ago. A Zen koan[182] suggests the same thing: "once upon a time there was no time"[179].

Quantum Theory[80] in physics suggests that the universe can have any possible history as opposed to a single history, a view that can be altered to allow for determinism[224], as suggested by Chen[223]. In quantum physics, a particle does not have definite position or velocity until it is measured by an observer. This view is at odds with classic reality, which assumes that objects are where they are whether we look at them or not.

The thinking of the pre-Socratic philosopher Heraclitus (circa 500 BCE) who pondered on the unity of opposites and observed that one cannot enter the same river twice (the river changes; the person changes) comes to mind.[229]

The basic unit of quantum information is the qubit[216], which is a two-state system (Superposition: the state of a particle is not defined for certain until it is measured[217]) Ultracold pairs of calcium fluoride molecules manipulated by laser beams have achieved entanglement (the states of two or more objects are described in reference to each other, even though they are spatially separated)[219], essential for a quantum information platform.[218]

There was an attempt to use **Quantum Mechanics**[81] which deals in statistical probability rather than certainty, to support a concept of dualistic consciousness: mind-body dualism: stating that mental phenomena are non-physical. The concept of quantum consciousness utilized the quantum mechanical phenomena of entanglement[82]: objects that must be described together even though they may be spatially separated, and superposition[83, 184]: a quantum system can exist in multiple states or configurations at the same time[176]. In quantum mechanics, particles are described by wave functions, which represent the probability distribution of their properties. Quantum objects ranging from photons to molecules have a dual nature of both particle and wave[177]. Wave functions may overlap. The system can be in a combination of states, with each state having a probability of being observed. However, when the system is observed or measured, it collapses into a single state.

Leonard Susskind in 2017 broached the possibility that there could be a close relationship between Quantum Mechanics and quantum gravity which might be shown by quantum computers. This was expressed as GR=QM[227], where GR stands for General Relativity (Einstein)[183] and QM represents Quantum Gravity. That proposed close relationship could bring the prospect of theory unification closer.

Quantum Mechanics led the physicist Hugh Everett to the quantum worlds[84] theory, proposing the existence of many non-communicating worlds.

Quantum Field Theory describes particulate matter as excitations in a field. Anthony Zee[230] states that quantum field theory "arose out of our need to describe the ephemeral nature of life". He makes the point that "particles can be born and particles can die".

Supersymmetry,[85] a precondition of Supergravity,[86] is a theoretical condition in which force and matter are two facets of the same thing. **Supergravity** is a quantum theory of gravity combining principles of supersymmetry and **General Relativity**[234] (Einstein) which conceptualizes the curvature of space-time. Gravity is a geometric property of space-time.[183]. Supergravity includes gravity with electromagnetic force and the weak and strong nuclear forces.[86] String Theory[20,21] which preceded the concept of supersymmetry, states that particles are patterns of vibration. What we see as solid is illusory. String Theory leads to consideration of a multidimensional universe[19].

Grand Unified Theory (GUT) of Physics

The **Standard Model** of physics elucidated how three (weak, electromagnetic, strong) of the four forces of nature interact with matter.[88] The Grand Unified Theory attempts to merge these three forces into one.[87]

Theory of Everything (TOE) is similarly a name for the unification of all four classes of natural forces- gravity, electromagnetism, strong nuclear force, weak nuclear force, which are probably artificially divided- into a single law compatible with quantum theory. TOE would include all forces and be able to predict all observations. M-theory[77] is a candidate to be the Theory of Everything. Jonathan Oppenheim is postulating how General Relativity could be reconciled with Quantum Theory.[215]

Red on White Circle | Jack Bush

Jack Bush (1909-1977)

Red On White Circle was included in the National Gallery of Canada's exhibition - A Jack Bush Retrospective 2014- 2015

...this painting has an almost cosmological sense...

Red on White Circle, 1961 © Estate of Jack Bush / CARCC Ottawa 2024

CHAPTER 9
THEORETICAL COALESCENCE: THE SERENITY HYPOTHESIS

Atomic Theory[66] has led us to the understanding that matter and energy are interchangeable. Einstein[23] came up with the curvature of space-time in his theory of General Relativity.[79] Matter and force are forms of the same thing.[85] What we see as solid is illusory.[20,21]

The division between the strong force, the weak force, electromagnetism and gravity is artificial,[19] calling for a Grand Unification Theory[87] compatible with Quantum Theory.[19,80.] Hawking and Mlodinow call this M-theory.[77] Panpsychism[60,61,62,63] proposes that the cosmos itself has a form of consciousness, proto-consciousness[61,89] which would be a most significant characteristic of the whole. There could be an aligning of a Grand Unified Theory of Physics with Panpsychism to create a Universal Understanding of our total cosmic environment.

It would also hearken back to mystics who respect natural objects, and to ancient persistent monotheistic beliefs that the Deity is a Unity.

The model-dependent realism[76] approach suggests theorizing or modeling based on sensory input to our brains. Judging from my own sensory experience, serenity: being at peace with oneself; is present when the inevitability of death is on the horizon. It is felt in major religions and philosophies that inner peace is possibly the highest form of consciousness. The innate expectancy of merging into cosmic consciousness could make one serene.

Serenity Hypothesis posits that with death we seamlessly enter into a serene peaceful state (state of grace[232]?) of cosmic consciousness.

If M-Theory[77,169], a Theory of Everything, a Grand Unification Theory[87] could be achieved to explain the physical world, and the cosmos itself has a proto-consciousness[60,61] into which we merge, we will have come a long way to understanding our cosmic environment and our relationship to it. M-theory itself is envisioned as a group of overlapping theories, so the possibility of a theory of cosmic proto-consciousness becoming part of that exists.

Astronomical Observations

The scientifically based, and still debated, perception that dark energy and dark matter make up the majority of matter-energy in the universe should bring us to the awareness that we have yet much to learn about our cosmic environment.[200]

Dark matter, discernible by its gravitational effect, does not give off, absorb or reflect electromagnetic radiation. Fritz Zwicky first proposed its existence, which was affirmed some forty years later by Vera Rubin and Kent Ford.[201]

An interesting phenomenon within the realm of astrophysics is the pulsatility of stars[90], including our own sun[91]. Quite a compelling analogy.

CHAPTER 10
WILDER PENFIELD MD: GETTING THE PICTURE STRAIGHT

I did meet Wilder Penfield,[92,93] a great thinker and preeminent twentieth century neurosurgeon who mapped the brain. His colleague in that endeavor was Herbert Jasper, one of the originals to study "brain waves", action potentials in neurons[94] (specialized nervous system cells that can be stimulated and conduct impulses) and to bring electroencephalogram (EEG) equipment into the operating room. The work they pioneered has continued to this day, now with the Human Connectome Project[95] which is mapping the connectivity of the brain.

As a nineteen year-old premedical student, I was informed that for consideration of my acceptance to medical school I was scheduled for an interview with Wilder Penfield. I was awestruck that this legendary icon was taking the time to meet with me. I could not even conceive of what questions he might ask, or what he might think of me.

I was the only student there at the appointed time. I remember the hushed silence. I was ushered into his inner office at the "Neuro" (Montreal Neurological Institute). The great man was standing on a chair, hanging a picture. He asked me if it was straight. I assured him that it was. I remember nothing else about our talk. I got into medical school. The picture was straight.

Wilder Penfield, as he mapped the brain, searched for the soul. He never found it. Despite that, he came to the conclusion that God exists. Part of that conclusion was based on his work with direct brain stimulation on patients who were awake. The brain itself has no direct pain receptors, although it processes the feelings of pain from everywhere in the body. Thus, neurosurgeons can operate on patients who are awake and comfortable. Through direct brain stimulation of specific areas, notably in the temporal lobes, Penfield was able to elicit specific sensations[92,96] but never abstract thought, leading to the conclusion that there is more to the mind than the brain. In that, his thinking was in line with Aristotle[65], who believed that the mind is not wholly material.

CHAPTER 11
MEDICINE: SCIENCE, ART, CALLING

Medicine is a Science: in actuality, the melding of many scientific disciplines. It is an Art, often in applying the science to the individual patient. In its purest form, it is a Calling: the healthcare professional puts the interest of the patient above her/his self-interest, as is strikingly shown by the selflessness globally of health care professionals and ancillary workers in a pandemic situation.

We now know that immortality can be conferred to cells. The cell[97] is the basic living microscopic structure in the human body. Each cell is surrounded by a cell membrane. Cells generally have a center, the nucleus[98], which is itself surrounded by a membrane. The nucleus contains the chromosomes[99], on which rest the genes[100].

The genome is the complete DNA sequence, the blueprint of us. The genotype is the individual genes of each person.

We do know that steps can be taken to slow down, and possibly even reverse, aging.[101]

We do know that our genetic blueprints, our DNA[34,35] (deoxyribonucleic acid) gets handed down for millennia.

We do now know that the telomere[44,45,46,101], the end of the DNA strand can be manipulated to shorten or prolong life via the enzyme telomerase[48,101]. We no longer cite any finite number as the ultimate age to which a human can live.

Advanced techniques are rapidly becoming available to prolong life and health in various medical conditions. Bioengineering[102] involves manufacturing recombinant DNA[36,37,38,39] and rearranging DNA[34,35]. Gene editing [103], a form of genetic engineering, involves insertion, deletion or replacement of DNA at a specific site by using CRISPR-Cas9[104].

CRISPR-Cas9 is a complex of RNA and protein (nucleases)[187] that recognizes the sequence of bases in a target gene. CRISPR–Cas9 is naturally part of the immune system, helping microorganisms combat viruses[214]. Cas9 (an enzyme) unwinds the double helix of DNA. The CRISPR RNA sequence binds to the target. Cas9 cuts both strands of the target DNA. In a modification, DNA sequences are not cut: the Cas9 enzyme carries a molecular switch that turns on target genes.

There is a CRISPR/Cas9 gene edited therapy for Sickle Cell Disease. The affected person's hematopoietic (blood-forming) stem cells, via CRISPR/Cas9, are modified and returned to the person. In the bone marrow these modified cells increase fetal hemoglobin production, preventing the red blood cells from sickling.[220]

Inserting a gene into cells to treat a disorder is known as gene therapy[105]. DNA mismatch repair[106] corrects errors of DNA replication. Tissue engineering[107] combines cells, scaffolding and biologically active molecules to create new tissue.

Somatic cell nuclear transfer essentially is therapeutic cloning. The nucleus is taken from an adult cell, and placed into an egg whose own nucleus has been removed. These embryonic stem cells are induced to form specialized cells (for example, heart muscle cells), that are needed by the very adult from whom the adult cell nucleus was originally taken. In other words, cells are made specifically for the person who needs them.

It may be becoming possible to predict disease severity[221] in an affected individual via machine learning: computers learning from data, utilizing statistics and algorithms.[222]

We do now know that intelligence does not peak at age twelve, and the prior theory that new brain cells, neurons, could no longer be produced, neurogenesis,[108] beyond that point, was not true.

We also know, that as much as we know, our collective knowledge barely scratches the surface.

"…this is not the end. It is not even the beginning of the end, but it is, perhaps, the end of the beginning." (Winston Churchill).[109] Those words could easily apply to our present level of knowledge in medicine and the sciences that underpin it, despite the logarithmic increase in our acquisition of knowledge. We need to allow the research to take us where it might, even if it means changing our preconceived ideas.

Medicine, historically largely art and mysticism, switched increasingly to science with the advent of the scientific method[71]. Medicine has benefited greatly from the current information explosion, with vast amounts of research being carried out, and from the largesse of people, businesses and governments who believe in the sanctity of the individual, and life. Translational Medicine[110], the mechanisms by which new drugs and tests get from the laboratory into the hands of medical personnel for administration to patients, and the mechanisms for ensuring that the populace gets necessary services, has become increasingly important. Medicine only becomes meaningful when patients actually receive beneficial new medications, and when patients actually receive necessary recommended services for optimal care. Getting beneficial new drugs made, then out of the labs and into the hands of doctors for administration to patients is the goal. The same is true for new medical devices. The next step is to ensure that the people who need the new drug or treatment, get it and hopefully use it. Health care workers should be prepared to educate patients utilizing their care concerning the need for a given device or medication, the downside of not using it, along with possible harmful side effects, and possible alternative treatments.

Surgery has advanced to minimally invasive surgery and robotic surgery in many instances.

Instead of a big incision, the surgeon uses a laparoscope to look inside the body, and delicate instruments are inserted through tiny incisions to perform the surgery. The surgeon looks at a video console to see the view of the internal organs obtained by a camera on the laparoscope.

Gynecologists were among the very first to utilize minimally invasive surgery via the laparoscope as an operative tool.

With advanced training, they become adept at repairing, and even removing, diseased organs and structures through very small incisions.

Surgeons have gone beyond removing diseased gall bladders and appendices this way, and now do bowel resections, cancer surgery, and even transplant surgery in some instances utilizing minimally invasive techniques.

Orthopedic surgeons use very small incisions to put scopes into joints to visualize damaged areas, and to repair ligaments using precision instruments.

Holography

Many people already know about holography, having seen it at high tech amusement parks: suddenly there is a projected image sitting next to you, giving the appearance of a three-dimensional person.

The scattered light from an object is captured, then illuminated by a beam. Multiple two-dimensional pictures are assembled into a three dimensional display. Holographic displays that will aid radiologists in diagnosis, and interventional radiologists and surgeons in treatment, are being developed.

The surgeon performing minimally invasive surgery works off a television (computer) monitor. The image is flat, in two dimensions, height and width. As surgeons, we have trained ourselves to interpret the flat images seen on the television screens in three dimensions, because of our experience in the real world, and our knowledge of the anatomy inside the body. For example, objects farther away seem smaller, so we interpret the smaller object on the television screen as being in the distance, unless we know by training and experience that it is, in fact a closer, but smaller object. Surgeons have to be expertly trained to interpret the "flat" images of the inside of what they see on the monitor as having depth—so that they can tell whether an organ or blood vessel, or an abnormality, is close or far, so that their instruments go exactly to the right place.

It is very helpful for the surgeon to have a three-dimensional image to work with, along with magnification, some of the great advantages of robotic surgery[209].

Robotic surgery is, and is not, being operated on by a robot. The brains and the hands behind the surgery ultimately belong to the human surgeon. The surgeon—at the console monitor screen—can be operating on a patient in the same room, or halfway around the world. The robotic system removes even the finest hard tremor that the surgeon may have, and allows the surgeon to operate with much finer, smaller instruments on small, delicate structures.

Vast strides are being made in techniques to ameliorate conditions that not too long ago were often essentially untreatable, or only treatable with great risk and uncertain results. Instead of going through full scale surgery to, say, open a blocked artery, interventional radiologists and cardiologists, using real time imaging, thread a sophisticated, tiny catheter into the vessel, and then inflate a balloon, opening it, or leave in a stent, which is a latticework structure that can be opened in the vessel like a scaffold, and remains in place after the catheter is removed. The vessel can be permanently held open, or a dissolvable stent can be used. After the stent dissolves, the vessel should stay open on its own.

Heart disease, with accumulation of arteriosclerotic plaque in the coronary arteries that bring the blood supply to heart muscle, can result in complete blockage of a coronary artery with resultant death of heart muscle: a heart attack.

Blood vessels in the brain can occlude, resulting in brain tissue death: a stroke.

Another form of stroke is caused by bleeding into the brain. It is essential that in the evaluation of a person who is exhibiting signs of a stroke that the differentiation between these two types of stroke be made, as the treatment for each type is different. In one case, the physician wants to reinitiate blood circulation to the affected area of brain, while in the other scenario bleeding must be stopped if possible.

Blood vessels in the lower limbs may clot. If a piece of that clot breaks off, and then travels through the bloodstream to a blood vessel supplying the lung, blocking it, this becomes the acute emergency of a pulmonary embolus. An embolus is an occluding substance that had its origin elsewhere and lodges in a blood vessel, occluding it.

In a seriously hemorrhaging patient, substances can be placed in the blood vessel supplying the bleeding site to block the vessel, stopping the bleeding.

Medicine has benefited from Information Technology, which has outmoded the paper medical chart and essentially made it a thing of the past.

Medical data will, going forward, be kept in a computer memory, with provisions made to safeguard confidentiality.

All your medical providers, physicians, and hospitals that you authorize will hopefully be able to instantly access your data, which will include all information concerning any surgical procedures you might have undergone, conditions you may have, and medications you might be taking. When seeing a physician, of course, you will have to describe any symptoms that might have developed since your last visit, so that the information can be updated in your database.

It is even possible to implant a computer chip with essential health information under a person's skin: (if we, as a society, decide we want to go there).

Physicians think in terms of diagnosing disease, then hopefully curing it. Disease is a defined term, as is Sickness. Disease[111] is an aberrant state of morphology or pathophysiology. Sickness[112] (illness) is an inability of individuals to pursue their goals and purposes because of impairments in function considered to be in the domain of medicine. Wellness is a neologism which basically means the preservation of good health.

This directional drive which is of great benefit to humanity, health, longevity and society at large does not leave much time or resources for reflection and study of matters that are outside the strict domain of the peer reviewed and provable in scientific terms.

At the same time, thinking professionals are constantly humbled by the vast complexity that is being discovered and uncovered, and by the flexibility of thought that is needed almost constantly as new discoveries supplant old beliefs.

I have always been struck by the way most terminally ill patients have approached death serenely with dignity and grace. This tends often to be in contrast with the understandable foreboding, fear and sense of imminent loss evident and expressed by their soon to be survivors. How do we explain this dichotomy? The scientific explanation might rest on the delivery of endogenous opioid peptides, endorphins[113] or exogenous substances to opioid receptors[114] in the brain of the terminally ill patient, or something more.

CHAPTER 12
THE PROLONGATION OF LIFE AND CONSCIOUSNESS; AGING AND ITS REVERSAL

We are demonstrably preserving consciousness as we know it by increasing lifespan. Medicine is concerned with the prolongation of human life, and the quality of that life. We now know how to prevent and cure many disease processes that afflict humanity. We are capable of turning other heretofore deadly diseases into manageable conditions. The science, including the knowledge of aging processes, is advancing rapidly.

Aging and its Reversal

It is becoming possible, at the level of the human cell, to prolong life, or reverse the aging process itself. Single cell biology[115], the study of the individual cell, has become a discipline.

Immortality of the living human cell is achievable. Ironically, cancer cell lines[116] have shown us that. An important, now generally known, issue is how such cell lines were initially obtained years ago. Genes in the cell control cell aging. Genes that cause cell death (apoptosis)[49] are known as self-destruct genes[117].

Some inherited genes predispose to life threatening diseases. Genetic manipulation, as outlined previously, is being developed to negate the effects of these predisposing genes. Some diseases are already being treated this way.

DNA[34,35], deoxyribonucleic acid, makes up the chromosomes[99] each of us inherits that carry the genes[100]. DNA is arranged in a distinctive double helix, three-dimensional pattern. It resembles a tight spiral staircase, with rungs (steps) each of which holds two (out of four) nucleic acid bases, called base pairs[118].

The end of each chromosome, made up of DNA, is called a telomere[44,45,46], which gives stability to the end of the chromosome, preventing abnormal recombinations[36,37,38,39] (mutations). The telomere is maintained and repaired by the enzyme telomerase[48]. An enzyme[47] is an organic catalyst. Enzymes facilitate chemical reactions within the human body. If telomerase is activated, a cell may be induced to become immortal. If telomerase is inhibited, cells die.

Every organ and tissue in the human body is made up of specialized cells. Specialized cells arise from the stem cells found in the early developing baby, the embryo. It is possible to grow new specialized organ and muscle cells from stem cells. A stem cell[119] is an undifferentiated cell that has the potential to become a specialized cell with a specific function, such as a blood cell or a muscle cell. Shinya Yamanaka, in his breakthrough work, described the use of four genes- the Yamanaka Factors- to reprogram adult cells into induced pluripotent (iPS) stem cells.[120,121] Induced (I) Pluripotent (P) Stem (S) cells are cells from an adult human that have been reprogrammed into an embryonic-like state. These cells can be used to regenerate damaged body organs. There are no issues of rejection of the cells, because they are derived from the very same person who needs them.[185, 186]

An injection of stem cells into the body to replace damaged or diseased tissue or blood is known as a stem cell transplant.[122]

Regenerative medicine[123] involves the creation of new organs, tissues, and body parts from stem cells, including one's own stem cells, which are placed on a dissolvable matrix, which is a framework, or scaffold, derived from animal tissue. This matrix is shaped into the body part that is to be reformed.

For example, the esophagus is the tube leading down from the mouth (oropharynx) to the stomach. Someone whose esophagus needs to be removed because of cancer, can get a new esophagus made from their very own cells.

Normal cells are placed on the matrix, which has been formed into the shape of the esophagus. The cells grow on the matrix. The matrix then dissolves, leaving a new human esophagus, made of the person's own cells. All the problems of transplant rejection are no longer of concern in this case, because the new esophagus is made up of the host person's own cells.

Heart valves can be made in this way, to replace leaking or damaged valves.

Theoretically, it is possible to build any organ or tissue in the human body in this way.

There has already been a case where the severed tip of a finger has been regrown normally.

This is tissue engineering.[107]

This is a great distance removed from my own experience with a similar case more than fifty years ago. An aircraft carrying the Nobel Prize-winning Prime Minister of Canada, Lester Pearson, was heading to our NORAD base in North Bay, Ontario. A steward on that plane was so nervous serving the Prime Minister that he (the steward) sliced off the tip of his own finger. Luckily, personnel on the aircraft had the presence of mind to keep the severed tip. I had fortuitously recently completed a surgical rotation with the then renowned hand surgeon Dr Martin Entin[228]. In the base operating room I was assisted by a Royal Canadian Airforce Medic, and was struck by his level of competence and training. I successfully reattached the severed tip. We sent the steward back on the aircraft to Ottawa with explicit instructions for postoperative care of the finger.

The entire field of organ transplantation[124], the replacement of hopelessly diseased organs by healthy ones will be revolutionized by the availability of new organs that will not be rejected by the body of the person needing the transplant.

Precision medicine[125] studies how the genomic variation in an individual or their disease (tumor sample) influences drug response. Specific mutations in a tumor are identified so that targeted therapy can be brought to bear.

Targeted therapy[126] may utilize drugs designed to reverse the effects of specific mutations. Drugs, such as monoclonal antibodies[127] that go to specific receptor sites on cells, prevent the use of those receptor sites by, for example, cancer cells. "Monoclonal" refers to the fact that the antibody protein is derived from one clone of cells, all of which are identical.

Recent studies seem to show that actual reversal of aging[128] can be brought about by regeneration of the thymus gland[129], which is a lymphoid gland of the immune system[130] located in the neck that produces T-Cells[131], and by restoration of the immune system. The immune system allows the body to ward off invasion by foreign substances including infectious agents. Cells including T-lymphocytes that go to infected sites are elaborated in bone marrow and other areas. Antibodies (immunoglobulins)[132] that target specific invaders (antigens[133]) circulate in the bloodstream. Infected areas drain through lymphatic channels to the lymph nodes[134], where invading organisms are processed.

Aging[135] is the gradual loss of physiological functions accompanied by increasing risk of mortality and decreasing fertility. The Rate of Aging[136] is the ratio between damage accumulation and compensatory mechanisms.

The reversal of aging has become a topic of discussion and significant research.

Epigenetics[137] is the study of the processes that regulate the turning on and off of genes.

Epigenetic Age

Your epigenetic age, as opposed to your chronological age that is marked by your birthdays, is determined by the extent and number of repairs to your DNA carried out by a process known as methylation. The more that repair work has been carried out to reverse oxidative damage, the older you are inferred to be. Ideally, your epigenetic age is less than your chronological age and partially explains why some people live longer than others.

The epigenome[138] describes all the chemical modifications to DNA and DNA-associated proteins in the cell which alter gene expression. Epigenetic changes can drive aging. Much of the epigenome is reset when the genome[139] is passed to off-spring. The genome is a person's complete DNA sequence. In fertilization, fusion of ovum and spermatozoon, the newly formed zygote[140] (fertilized cell) has forty-six chromosomes[99] arranged in twenty-three pairs, with one chromosome of each pair derived from the mother, and one from the father. The chromosomes, which carry the genes[100], are made up of DNA.

Epigenetic reprogramming is being worked on, with the goal of achieving rejuvenation[225]. .Much of this work follows on Yamanaka's landmark work, creating pluripotent stem cells from adult tissue.[121,226]

Maurice Michel, Karolinska Institute, working on artificial functions of DNA repair enzymes for the treatment of disease. has shown that a small molecule binding to the site of a DNA repair enzyme can increase its activity, leading to enhanced DNA repair after oxidative damage.[211]

Sirtuin genes exert an anti-aging effect in yeast. Increased sirtuin activity may be related to the mechanism by which caloric restriction extends life span[141].

Geroscience[142,143] studies the intersection of aging, biology, chronic disease and health.

Geroprotectors,[144] drugs that will target the fundamental mechanisms of aging, are sought.

Senolytics[145] are drugs that kill senescent (old), non-dividing cells that accumulate in aging organs.[197]

Green Spot | Ellen Altfest

https://www.whitecube.com/gallery-exhibitions/green-spot

https://hillslife.jp/art/2022/07/22/painter-at-work

The eminent internationally acclaimed and exhibited artist Ellen Altfest lives and works in the southern United States.

Her work entitled Green Spot is featured here. Its exquisitely meticulous, painstakingly created, hand painted representation of lichen evokes Quantum Theory concepts of supersymmetry and entanglement, or a neural network.

Ellen's upcoming exhibition starts at the Frist Museum, in Nashville TN.

Green Spot © Ellen Altfest. Photo © White Cube (Christopher Burke, New York)

CHAPTER 13

THE NEURODEGENERATION DILEMMA

As longevity increases, largely due to major advances in medical care and its delivery, there is a concomitant increase in the incidence of neurodegenerative disorders[146]. With aging itself, there tends to be a progressive loss of brain function, with demonstrable loss of cerebral cortex[147] of the brain on imaging.

Alzheimer's Disease[148,149] is a prominent neurodegenerative problem leading to dementia,[150] a loss of cognitive functioning. We do not yet have the answers, either as to etiology (cause) or definitive treatment of such conditions prevalent in older persons that affect cognition[151], the conscious mental activities of thinking, learning, understanding and remembering.

Hallmarks of the pathogenesis of Alzheimer's Disease are accumulation in the brain of beta amyloid[152] that clumps in amorphous plaques, and Tau protein[153]. Medications that can lessen the amyloid burden have been given accelerated approval by the FDA in the USA.[173,174]

Terminal lucidity[235], when it occurs, can be quite dramatic. Communication skills and connectedness reappear. A person may suddenly recall heretofore forgotten names and faces, and express desires, say, for food, shortly before death. This phenomenon is difficult to study, as it is unexpected, relatively short lived and occurs unpredictably in some cognitively impaired persons. Unproven possible explanations of this phenomenon have even included allusions to an afterlife. A more mundane explanation is that terminal lucidity is simply **paradoxical lucidity**[236] that coincidentally is triggered near the time of death, with some recollection occurring possibly in conjunction with the constant presence of loved ones. It is well known that Alzheimer's afflicted persons may have occasional episodes of recognition at seemingly random times (paradoxical lucidity). The reasons for this are unknown.

Mild Cognitive Impairment (MCI)[154] is a dysfunction of conscious mental activities with minimal impairment of the instrumental activities of daily living (IADL)[213] that allow an individual to live independently in the community. The more basic activities of daily living (ADLS)[212] include feeding, dressing, bathing and walking.

In Amnestic MCI memory dysfunction predominates. There can be progression to dementia.

The universal indefinite or eternal persistence of human consciousness could pose moral, ethical and even logistical questions, especially in view of the increasing, but not uniform, prominence of cognitive decline.

It would be naïve to suggest that everyone could enter a state of eternal consciousness at the height of their cognitive powers. As society ages, the incidence of cognitive decline increases. This would lead to massive discrepancies in awareness.

The **Serenity Hypothesis** and proto-consciousness (primordial consciousness) of the cosmos solves this dilemma: we uniformly enter into the universality of the proto-consciousness of the cosmos in a serene state. Moreover, if achieving a serene, blissful state is indeed the best anyone could aspire to, then this would be an enviable prospect.

CHAPTER 14
ARTIFICIAL INTELLIGENCE (AI)

We can approach the consciousness question from the opposite pole, that is, how do we create consciousness, or let consciousness arise spontaneously by creating what we perceive as the necessary conditions for its appearance? If we learn that, we would be in a much better position to ascertain the presence of extracorporeal consciousness.

Artificial Intelligence[155,156] involves the utilization of computer systems able to perform tasks normally attributable to human intelligence. These include visual perception, speech recognition, decision-making and language translation. Ideally, the computer systems would think and act humanly and rationally. AI utilizes **Machine Learning**[157,158] in which data is fed to a computer and statistical techniques are used to help the computer get better at a task without specifically programming it for that. Machine Learning operates at the intersection of computing algorithms and statistics. **Deep Learning**[159,160,199] is a type of machine learning that runs data inputs through multiple layers of biologically inspired neural network architecture, enabling prediction of outcomes when new data is presented.

AI is increasingly being utilized in medical research, in the development of novel proteins, vaccines, and possible treatments.[196]

Neuromorphic engineering[161] involves designing hardware and physical models of neural and sensory systems.

At what point will Artificial Intelligence applications become life? As long as we are adept enough to keep redefining life, we can put off that day. By introducing metabolism into the definition of life, that precludes the majority of machines that do not work that way from being considered life forms.

Reverse Perspective | Kim Keever

https://www.kimkeever.com

"I have often thought about the *consciousness* of animals. I consider myself an 'armchair naturalist'. I originally majored in biology but went on to graduate in engineering. (and worked at NASA)

One of my favorite examples is the 'pronking' of young gazelles showing off their vitality vs the older gazelles which may live 10 to 12 years. Just as we all feel our physical prowess decline as we get older, I can only imagine that herd animals must feel the same as they get older and see their older herd members fall prey to lions and hyenas."

Keever's artistic statement on how we perceive things comes boldly to the fore here.

Kim Keever, *Reverse Perspective*
https://www.kimkeever.com

CHAPTER 15
THEORIES OF CONSCIOUSNESS

Assembly Theory: The recently elucidated Assembly Theory posits that "life is the only physics that generates complex objects" and that these objects (are) so complex the only physical mechanism to form them is evolution." A key element is Time: it takes unidirectional time for such complex systems to form and come to fruition.[175]

The complexity of the system is measured by an **Assembly Index** which describes the number of steps needed to reach a given state in a molecule. Greater than fifteen steps have only been found in living samples.

The proponents of Assembly Theory define the threshold at which life arises from non-life as the ability of complex molecules to use information to make copies of themselves.

There are many largely unproven theories of consciousness, including **IIT**, the **integrated information theory**,[202, 203, 207] that proposes consciousness starts with experience of phenomena[206] and emerges from the way information is processed within networks of neurons. Systems that are most interconnected[207], involving feedback loops and integrating information, may achieve consciousness.

Other theories include **GNW**[204]**, the global neuronal workspace theory** that proposes in the conscious state, network ignition associated and recurrent processing amplify a neural representation, allowing the information to be globally accessed by local processors.

The **recurrent processing theory**[205] ties perceptual consciousness to recurrent activity in interconnected sensory areas with feedback mechanisms.

The **higher-order thought theory**[205] intuitively suggests that to be in a conscious state, one must be aware of it. This theory alludes to activity in the prefrontal cortex of the brain. Some or all of these theories may be complementary.

On the other hand, if the question is reframed: at what point does consciousness[61] arise spontaneously in a machine? The argument has been made that if a system is complex enough, and can get input from environmental stimuli, it can come to conclusions (decisions) that is, make a choice we could not necessarily predict that would be indistinguishable from free will. Does that constitute self-awareness, which is consciousness?

Consciousness is not static. It is a dynamic, constantly subtly shifting state, dependent on sensory input interacting with accumulated knowledge and experience. Our sensory input is visual, auditory and tactile. Smell and taste are involved as well. It is dependent on our sleep/wake cycle and metabolic factors such as our glucose level and state of hydration.

Artificial intelligence at this stage is dependent upon us, not only for inputting existing information at a given time, but also for being its sense organs, for example by collectively and constantly posting the observations gained through our senses on the Cloud via social media and our various devices. Given that AI has the potential, for example, to get data input from "visual" sources that we have created with a far greater spectrum and range than the human eye, and auditory sources that we have created with a far greater spectrum and range than the human ear, and given AI's speed, computing power and interconnectedness , we may have more immediate issues (and benefits) to deal with than defining AI consciousness.

If we reach the point where we can transfer our consciousness along with our knowledge to a machine, then the question of whether post-death consciousness can and does exist may become less pressing, even moot. That machine, in order to maintain a conscious state, would again need sensory and data input in order to maintain a dynamic consciousness. That evolving consciousness would eventually become far removed from our initial input, making our effort somewhat futile on at least some level.

CHAPTER 16
SUBJECTIVE EXPERIENCE

In the end, we tend to be guided by our own subjective experience and may only get real knowledge when we approach that intersection between life and death, much like those watchers who gather on the Caribbean shore at sunset, to intently watch the sun disappear beneath the horizon, and catch that unmistakable but very fleeting blue flash, the final observable event.

At age eleven, 1949, I underwent emergency appendectomy, which was no small thing in that era. Ether droplet anesthesia via cheesecloth over a strainer was utilized. To this day I vividly recall a pinwheel of spinning lights, which could be attributed to asphyxia.

In 1970 I took a Mercedes test drive on the Trans-Canada Highway with a professional racing driver. He came off an exit ramp at speed and flipped the big sedan over a retaining fence. We landed back on the highway on the roof. I crawled out a broken window and supported myself on the overturned chassis with outstretched arms to enable breathing due to my broken ribs. I do not remember transport to the Montreal Neurological Institute (the "Neuro") but I do remember awakening there in a state of serenity and peace. I felt no pain. There was a magnificent abstract painting on the wall, a multitude of pixels of varied color, facing the foot of my bed. I do not remember the removal of broken glass from my eye, nor the care for my fractured ribs. The neurologic diagnosis was concussion,[162,] a traumatic injury to the brain[163].

I do remember at discharge being disappointed when I realized the abstract painting I had taken so much pleasure in was a mundane landscape.

In 2005 I underwent insertion of a cardiac stent. Immediately postoperatively I developed a femoral hematoma, an accumulation of blood at the site in my upper leg around the femoral artery where the catheter had initially been placed to insert the stent into my coronary artery. My blood pressure dropped, and I slipped into unconsciousness. I remember the lead physician resuscitating me repeatedly saying "Stay with me". I remember being in a serene state, trying, but not very hard, to open my eyes occasionally: I liked the peaceful serene state I was in.

In 2007, I suddenly felt faint while walking on the street. I started to sit down on a bench. I awoke in an emergency room bed at New York Hospital (now New York Presbyterian Weill Cornell campus) with that now familiar deep feeling of serenity.

I had what could be described as a Near Death Experience[164] in 2008, when I developed bleeding into the sac around my heart (hemopericardium), cardiac tamponade[165] (inability of the heart to beat properly due to external pressure) and pulsus paradoxus[166,167]. I remember giving permission before surgery for medical students to observe and palpate the relatively rare jugular venous distension in my neck with inspiration. I was watching them from a distance. They were solemn and seemed frightened; I was deeply serene and remained that way while awake during the procedure and subsequently.

In 2019 while walking my perception became a series of still shots rather than a continuum. I remember reaching out to a balustrade. I awoke much later, in a deep state of serenity, in the hospital. There was no apprehension and no fear. After multitudinous tests a presumptive diagnosis of exclusion of transient ischemic arteriospasm (TIA)[168] with temporarily insufficient oxygenation of the brain was made.

As I write this, I am looking out over the deep rose color atop the distant hills in the west where the sun has just set. A pair of red-tailed hawks are nesting under the eaves of my home. I watch one as it soars away. They always return. I understand my medical history and I am serene.

SERENITY HYPOTHESIS
REFERENCES, LINKS

1. Esposito, Ron: Pathways to Serenity 2008 http://www.goconscious.com/home/articles/pathways_to_serenity.html

2. Sri Chinmoy: Bhaki Yoga: https://www.srichinmoy.org/resources/talks/meditation/inner_teaching

3. Nirvana; Buddhism: https://tricycle.org/magazine/nirvana-2/

4. Caplan, Ronald M: Consciousness: Glossary. The Care of the Older Person Fifth Edition, CRC Press, 2023 https://routledge.pub/The-Care-of-the-Older-Person https://careoftheolderperson.com

5. Tononi, G, Information Integration Theory of Consciousness https://bmcneurosci.biomedcentral.com/articles/10.1186/1471-2202-5-42

6. Neuroscience of Consciousness https://plato.stanford.edu/entries/consciousnessneuroscience/

7. Hippocrates: the forefather of neurology Neurol Sci 35(9):1349-52. Sep,2014 https://pubmed.ncbi.nlm.nih.gov/25027011/

8. Caplan, Ronald M: Coma: Glossary. The Care of the Older Person Fifth Edition, CRC Press, 2023 https://routledge.pub/The-Care-of-the-Older-Person https://careoftheolderperson.com

9. Collective consciousness https://www.thoughtco.com/collective-consciousnessdefinition-3026118

10. James, William: https://www.cambridge.org/core/books/cosmic consciousness/4637556D282954CAC81B1007B94F684E

11. James, William: https://www.brainpickings.org/2018/06/04/william-james-varietiesconsciousness/

12. James, William: The Varieties of Religious Experience: https://www.gutenberg.org/files/621/621-pdf.pdf

13. Cosmic Consciousness https://www.brainpickings.org/2019/04/11/cosmicconsciousness-maurice-bucke/

14. Edward Carpenter: The Art of Creation: Essays: https://www.goodreads.com/book/show/7551320-the-art-of-creation

15. Bucke and cosmic consciousness https://www.encyclopedia.com/philosophy-andreligion/other-religious-beliefs-and-general-terms/miscellaneous-religion/cosmicconsciousness

16. Cosmic Consciousness in Transcendental Meditation https://tmhome.com/booksvideos/7-states-of-consciousness-video-interview/

17. Hearing Range https://www.google.com/search?q=human+hearing+range&rlz=1C1CHBF_enUS821US8 21&oq=human+hearing+ran&aqs=chrome.1.69i57j0i433j0l3j0i395l3.198351j1j4&sourceid=chrome&ie=UTF-8

18. Time-Space Continuum https://einstein.stanford.edu/content/relativity/q411.html

19. Hawking, Stephen; Mlodinow, Leonard: Multiple Dimensions, Pages 85-120, Chapter 5: The Theory of Everything; The Grand Design. Bantam Books. 2010

20. Hawking, Stephen; Mlodinow, Leonard: String Theory, Pages 85-120, Chapter 5: The Theory of Everything; The Grand Design Bantam Books.2010 https://www.google.com/search?q=the+grand+design+stephen+hawking+pdf&rlz=1C1CHBF_enUS821US821&oq=the+grand+design+&aqs=chrome.3.46j0l4j69i57j0j69i64.16666j1j4&sourceid=chrome&ie=UTF-8

21. String Theory and Multiple Dimensions https://www.space.com/more-universedimensions-for-string-theory.html

22. Descartes, Rene Discourse on Method https://www.gutenberg.org/files/59/59-h/59-h.htm

23. Einstein, Albert https://www.researchgate.net/publication/279646461_Einstein_and_the_Atomic_Theory

24. Maynard, Susan The Illumination of Dr Bucke https://theilluminationofdrbucke.com/the-universe/

26. Genesis:1 Bible, King James Version https://quod.lib.umich.edu/cgi/k/kjv/kjvidx?type=DIV1&byte=1477

27. Chateau Frontenac https://www.hauntedplaces.org/item/chateau-frontenac/c

28. Entropy: Measurement of molecular disorder or randomness in a system. https://www.britannica.com/science/entropy-physics

29. Life https://www.google.com/search?rlz=1C1CHBF_enUS821US821&sxsrf=ALeKk007mA8gEJ fS83a8KXD_XDCjMxHuOg%3A1600519500079&ei=TP1lX_2yBK-xytMPyqa7yAo&q=life+definition&oq=+life+definition&gs_lcp=CgZwc3ktYWIQARgAMgwIABCxAxBDEEYQ-QEyBggAEAcQHjIGC

30. Death https://jamanetwork.com/journals/jama/fullarticle/2769148?guestAccessKey=c234904b-79e4-4fa8-970edbac5739205a&utm_source=silverchair&utm_campaign=jama_network&utm_content= ped_weekly_highlights&cmp=1&utm_medium=email

31. Death https://jamanetwork.com/journals/jama/articleabstract/2769149?guestAccessKey=002dcb34-be0f-4f21-986b-a78ed29ccb96&utm_source=silverchair&utm_campaign=jama_network&utm_content= ped_weekly_highlights&cmp=1&utm_medium=email

32. Clarfield, A. Mark: The role of religious belief in the end of life care of older persons: The Care of the Older Person Fifth Edition, CRC Press, 2023 https://routledge.pub/The-Careof-the-Older-Person https://careoftheolderperson.com

33. Darwin, Charles. On the Origin of the Species http://darwin online.org.uk/converted/pdf/1861_OriginNY_F382.pdf

34. Caplan, Ronald M: DNA: Glossary. The Care of the Older Person Fifth Edition. CRC Press, 2023 https://routledge.pub/The-Care-of-the-Older-Person https://careoftheolderperson.com

35. DNA: https://www.genome.gov/25520880/deoxyribonucleic-acid-dna-fact-sheet/

36. Caplan, Ronald M: Recombination: Glossary. The Care of the Older Person Fifth Edition. CRC Press, 2023 https://routledge.pub/The-Care-of-the-Older-Person https://careoftheolderperson.com

37. Recombination https://www.nature.com/scitable/topicpage/dna-is-constantlychanging-through-the-process-6524876

38. Caplan, Ronald M: Recombinant DNA Technology: Glossary. The Care of the Older Person Fifth Edition. CRC Press, 2023 https://routledge.pub/The-Care-of-the-OlderPerson https://careoftheolderperson.com

39. Recombinant DNA https://en.wikipedia.org/wiki/Recombinant_DNA

40. Magnetic Resonance Imaging (MRI) https://onlinelibrary.wiley.com/doi/full/10.1002/jmri.23642

41. Caplan, Ronald M: CAT Scan (Computerized Axial Tomography): Glossary. The Care of the Older Person Fifth Edition. CRC Press, 2023 https://routledge.pub/The-Care-of-theOlder-Person https://careoftheolderperson.com

42. Caplan, Ronald M: PET Scan (Positron Emission Tomography): Glossary, The Care of the Older Person Fifth Edition. CRC Press, 2023 https://routledge.pub/The-Care-of-theOlder-Person https://careoftheolderperson.com

43. Caplan, Ronald M: Receptor Site: Glossary, The Care of the Older Person Fifth Edition. CRC Press, 2023 https://routledge.pub/The-Care-of-the-Older-Person https://careoftheolderperson.com

44. Morais, Jose: Telomere: Introduction, The Care of the Older Person Fifth Edition. CRC Press, 2023 https://routledge.pub/The-Care-of-the-Older-Person https://careoftheolderperson.com

45. Caplan, Ronald M: Telomere: Glossary, The Care of the Older Person Fifth Edition, CRC Press, 2023 https://routledge.pub/The-Care-of-the-Older-Person https://careoftheolderperson.com

46. Telomere https://link.springer.com/article/10.1007/s10815-017-0967-6/fulltext.html?wt_mc=alerts.TOCjournals

47. Enzyme https://www.mcat.me/review/bb/enzyme-structure-and-function/

48. Telomerase http://study.com/academy/lesson/what-is-telomerase-definition-functionstructure.html

49. Programmed cell death (Apoptosis) http://www.ncbi.nlm.nih.gov/pmc/articles/PMC2117903/

50. Glasnost https://www.britannica.com/topic/glasnost

51. Sagan, Carl: The Varieties of Scientific Experience: A Personal View of the Search for God https://www.brainpickings.org/2013/12/20/carl-sagan-varieties-of-scientificexperience/

52. Sagan, Carl: Interview https://uscatholic.org/articles/198105/god-and-carl-sagan-is-thecosmos-big-enough-for-both-of-them/

53. Lecker, Sidney: Biofeedback, p.195-199. The Natural Way to Stress Control. Grosset & Dunlap. 1978

54. Harley, Jack: Self-Hypnosis https://www.mindsethealth.com/matter/self-hypnosis

55. Brown, Richard: Donald O. Hebb and the Organization of Behavior https://molecularbrain.biomedcentral.com/articles/10.1186/s13041-020-00567-8

56. Psychoanalysis https://www.health.harvard.edu/newsletter_article/Psychoanalysis_Theory_and_treatment

57. Regression Therapy https://psi-encyclopedia.spc.ac.uk/articles/regression-therapy

58. Hypnosis https://www.health.harvard.edu/newsletter_article/Hypnosis_as_mental health_therapy

59. Task Force on Emergency Response and Preparedness, President's Commission on the Accident at Three Mile Island http://large.stanford.edu/courses/2012/ph241/tran1/docs/188.pdf

60. Matloff Gregory; Can Panpsychism become an observational science? https://jcer.com/index.php/jcj/article/view/579/595

61. Wheeler, John Archibald, Penrose, Roger, Koch, Christof: Proto-consciousness https://bigthink.com/philip-perry/the-universe-may-be-conscious-prominent-scientistsstate

62. Kleiner, Tull: Integrated Information Theory https://arxiv.org/abs/2002.07655

63. Kleiner, Johannes: Models of Consciousness https://www.semanticscholar.org/paper/Models-of-Consciousness-Kleiner/7d25fbbc709c7d20f98894a30d79e0755c2f61c2

64. Tononi, Guilio Integrated Information Theory (IIT) 2004 http://www.scholarpedia.org/article/Integrated_information_theory

65. Aristotle: The mind: part of the soul https://plato.stanford.edu/entries/aristotlepsychology/

66. Atomic Theory Timeline https://www.barcodesinc.com/articles/timeline-on-atomicstructure.htm

67. Dalton, John https://www.universetoday.com/38169/john-daltons-atomic-model/

68. Rutherford, Ernest https://www.sciencehistory.org/historical-profile/ernest-rutherford

69. Bohr, Niels http://abyss.uoregon.edu/~js/glossary/bohr_atom.html

70. Oppenheimer, J. Robert https://www.nationalww2museum.org/war/articles/makingthe-atomic-bomb-trinity-test

71. Scientific Method https://plato.stanford.edu/entries/scientific-method/

72. Inductive and Deductive Reasoning Inductive (theory development) reasoning and deductive (testing theory)reasoning https://www.google.com/search?q=inductive+reasoning+vs+deductive+reasoning&rlz=1C1CHBF_enUS821US821&oq=inductive+reasoning&aqs=chrome.2.69i57j0i433j0l2j0i395l4.11968j1j4&sourceid=chrome&ie=UTF-8

73. Hypothesis: proposed explanation, prediction; Theory: Substantial explanation of an occurrence https://www.google.com/search?q=hypothesis+vs+theory&rlz=1C1CHBF_enUS821US821&oq=hypothesis+&aqs=chrome.2.69i57j0i67i433l2j0i67i395i433l2j0i67i395l2j0i67i395i433.16745j1j4&sourceid=chrome&ie=UTF-8

74. Rational Thinking as a Process http://www.ascd.org/publications/books/101017/chapters/Rational-Thinking-as-aProcess.aspx#:~:text=Rational%20thinking%20is%20the%20ability,arrive%20at%20a%20 sound%20conclusion.

75. Rationalism vs Empiricism https://plato.stanford.edu/entries/rationalismempiricism/#IntuThes

76. Hawking, Stephen; Mlodinow, Leonard: Model-Dependent Realism; Pages 3-12, Chapter 1: The Mystery of Being; The Grand Design. Bantam Books 2010

77. Hawking, Stephen; Mlodinow, Leonard: M-Theory; Pages 3-12, Chapter 1: The Mystery of Being; The Grand Design. Bantam Books 2010

78. Hawking, Stephen; Mlodinow, Leonard: Big Bang Theory; Pages 32-60, Chapter 3: What is Reality?; The Grand Design. Bantam Books 2010

79. Siegel, Ethan General Relativity, Big Bang Forbes https://www.forbes.com/sites/startswithabang/2019/12/04/this-is-why-scientists-willnever-exactly-solve-general-relativity/?sh=6c83720834a8

80. Hawking, Stephen; Mlodinow, Leonard: Quantum Theory; Chapter 1: Pages 3-12, The Mystery of Being; The Grand Design. Bantam Books 2010

81. Quantum Mechanics https://www.livescience.com/33816-quantum-mechanicsexplanation.html

82. Quantum Entanglement https://www.sciencedaily.com/terms/quantum_entanglement.htm

83. The Superposition Principle in Quantum Mechanics: Dass, N D Hari https://www.researchgate.net/publication/258566887_The_Superposition_Principle_in_Quantum_Mechanics_-_did_the_rock_enter_the_foundation_surreptitiously

84. Quantum Worlds theory https://www.nature.com/articles/d41586-019-02602-8

85. Supersymmetry http://hitoshi.berkeley.edu/public_html/susy/susy.html

86. Supergravity https://www.hindawi.com/journals/ahep/2016/3595120/

87. Krauss, Lawrence: A Brief History of the Grand Unified Theory of Physics https://nautil.us/issue/46/balance/a-brief-history-of-the-grand-unified-theory-ofphysics

88. Standard Model https://home.cern/science/physics/standard-model

89. Hobson, J Allan: REM sleep and proto-consciousness https://pubmed.ncbi.nlm.nih.gov/19794431/

90. Pulsatile Stars: https://astronomy.com/magazine/news/2020/07/how-pulsating-starsunlock-our-universe

91. Pusatile Sun: https://ase.tufts.edu/cosmos/print_images.asp?id=25

92. Egnor, Michael: Penfield https://evolutionnews.org/2016/04/wilder_penfield/

93. Penfield Bio https://www.mcgill.ca/neuro/about/wilder-graves-penfield

94. Neuron: http://www.ncbi.nlm.nih.gov/books/NBK21535/ https://www.nature.com/articles/s41593-01802052.epdf?shared_access_token=60bklwIRkphHPPY3R_u069RgN0jAjWel9jnR3ZoTv0M_ZnMCyHI8KbNyV63mNxsudkNYBmXFIhQDgOHiquMVMmq6S_Ta_jrenQf

95. Human Connectome Project: http://www.humanconnectome-project.org/

96. Penfield: temporal lobe stimulation with out-of-body experience https://www.cell.com/trends/cognitive-sciences/fulltext/S1364-6613(03)00027-5

97. Caplan, Ronald M: Cell: Glossary, The Care of the Older Person Fifth Edition. CRC Press, 2023 https://routledge.pub/The-Care-of-the-Older-Person https://careoftheolderperson.com

98. Caplan, Ronald M: Nucleus: Glossary, The Care of the Older Person Fifth Edition. CRC Press, 2023 https://routledge.pub/The-Care-of-the-Older-Person https://careoftheolderperson.com

99. Caplan, Ronald M: Chromosome: Glossary, The Care of the Older Person Fifth Edition. CRC Press, 2023 https://routledge.pub/The-Care-of-the-Older-Person https://careoftheolderperson.com

100. Caplan, Ronald M: Gene: Glossary, The Care of the Older Person Fifth Edition. CRC Press, 2023 https://routledge.pub/The-Care-of-the-Older-Person https://careoftheolderperson.com

101. Caplan, Ronald M: Aging (possible reversal) Preface, Pages vii-viii. Long Life Strategy, RMC Publishing, LLC www.rmcpublishingllc.com

102. Bioengineering http://www.mdpi.com/journal/bioengineering

103. Caplan, Ronald M: Gene Editing: Glossary, The Care of the Older Person Fifth Edition. CRC Press, 2023 https://routledge.pub/The-Care-of-the-Older-Person https://careoftheolderperson.com

104. Caplan, Ronald M: CRISPR-Cas9: Glossary, The Care of the Older Person Fifth Edition. CRC Press, 2023 https://routledge.pub/The-Care-of-the-Older-Person https://careoftheolderperson.com

105. Caplan, Ronald M: Gene Therapy: Glossary, The Care of the Older Person Fifth Edition. CRC Press, 2023 https://routledge.pub/The-Care-of-the-Older-Person https://careoftheolderperson.com

106. Caplan, Ronald M: DNA Mismatch Repair: Glossary, The Care of the Older Person Fifth Edition. CRC Press, 2023 https://routledge.pub/The-Care-of-the-Older-Person https://careoftheolderperson.com

107. Caplan, Ronald M: Tissue Engineering: Glossary, The Care of the Older Person Fifth Edition. CRC Press, 2023 https://routledge.pub/The-Care-of-the-Older-Person https://careoftheolderperson.com

108. Caplan, Ronald M: Neurogenesis: Glossary, The Care of the Older Person Fifth Edition. CRC Press, 2023 https://routledge.pub/The-Care-of-the-Older-Person https://careoftheolderperson.com

109. Churchill, Winston http://www.churchill-society-london.org.uk/EndoBegn.html

110. Caplan, Ronald M: Translational Medicine: Glossary, The Care of the Older Person Fifth Edition. CRC Press, 2023 https://routledge.pub/The-Care-of-the-Older-Person https://careoftheolderperson.com

111. Boudreau, JD, Cassell, EJ, Fuks, A: Disease: Chapt.1, page 5: Physicianship and the Rebirth of Medical Education Oxford University Press 2018

112. Boudreau, JD, Cassell, EJ, Fuks, A: Sickness: Chapt.1, page 5; Chapt.2, Page 21: Physicianship and the Rebirth of Medical Education. Oxford University Press 2018

113. Caplan, Ronald M: Endorphins: Glossary, The Care of the Older Person Fifth Edition. CRC Press, 2023 https://routledge.pub/The-Care-of-the-Older-Person https://careoftheolderperson.com

114. Caplan, Ronald M: Opioid: Glossary, The Care of the Older Person Fifth Edition. CRC Press, 2023 https://routledge.pub/The-Care-of-the-Older-Person https://careoftheolderperson.com

115. Caplan, Ronald M: Single Cell Biology: Glossary, The Care of the Older Person Fifth Edition. CRC Press, 2023 https://routledge.pub/The-Care-of-the-Older-Person https://careoftheolderperson.com

116. Cancer Cell Lines https://www.ncbi.nlm.nih.gov/pmc/articles/PMC6721418/

117. Caplan, Ronald M: Self-destruct genes: Glossary, The Care of the Older Person Fifth Edition. CRC Press, 2023 https://routledge.pub/The-Care-of-the-Older-Person https://careoftheolderperson.com

118. Caplan, Ronald M: Base pairs: Glossary, The Care of the Older Person Fifth Edition, CRC Press, 2023 https://routledge.pub/The-Care-of-the-Older-Person https://careoftheolderperson.com

119. Caplan, Ronald M: Stem cell: Glossary, The Care of the Older Person Fifth Edition. CRC Press, 2023 https://routledge.pub/The-Care-of-the-Older-Person https://careoftheolderperson.com

120. Induced Pluripotent Stem Cells https://hsci.harvard.edu/news/are-embryonic-stemcells-and-artificial-stem-cells-equivalent

121. Yamanaka factors https://pubmed.ncbi.nlm.nih.gov/19030024/

122. Caplan, Ronald M: Stem cell transplant: Glossary, The Care of the Older Person Fifth Edition. CRC Press, 2023 https://routledge.pub/The-Care-of-the-Older-Person https://careoftheolderperson.com

123. Caplan, Ronald M: Regenerative medicine: Glossary, The Care of the Older Person Fifth Edition. CRC Press, 2023 https://routledge.pub/The-Care-of-the-Older-Person https://careoftheolderperson.com

124. Caplan, Ronald M: Transplantation: Glossary, The Care of the Older Person Fifth Edition. CRC Press, 2023 https://routledge.pub/The-Care-of-the-Older-Person https://careoftheolderperson.com

125. Caplan, Ronald M: Precision Medicine:Glossary, The Care of the Older Person Fifth Edition. CRC Press, 2023 https://routledge.pub/The-Care-of-the-Older-Person https://careoftheolderperson.com

126. Targeted Therapy http://www.ncbi.nlm.nih.gov/pubmed/23470539

127. Caplan, Ronald M: Monoclonal Antibody: Glossary, The Care of the Older Person Fifth Edition. CRC Press, 2023 https://routledge.pub/The-Care-of-the-Older-Person https://careoftheolderperson.com

128. Caplan, Ronald M: Can Aging be Reversed? Long Life Strategy: Chapter 2, pages 40-42. RMC Publishing LLC 2020 www.rmcpublishingllc.com

129. Caplan, Ronald M: Thymus gland: Glossary, The Care of the Older Person Fifth Edition. CRC Press, 2023 https://routledge.pub/The-Care-of-the-Older-Person https://careoftheolderperson.com

130. Caplan, Ronald M: Immune system: Glossary, The Care of the Older Person Fifth Edition. CRC Press, 2023 https://routledge.pub/The-Care-of-the-Older-Person https://careoftheolderperson.com

131. Caplan, Ronald M: T-lymphocyte: Glossary, The Care of the Older Person Fifth Edition. CRC Press, 2023 https://routledge.pub/The-Care-of-the-Older-Person https://careoftheolderperson.com

132. Caplan, Ronald M: Antibody: Glossary, The Care of the Older Person Fifth Edition. CRC Press, 2023 https://routledge.pub/The-Care-of-the-Older-Person https://careoftheolderperson.com

133. Caplan, Ronald M: Antigen: Glossary, The Care of the Older Person Fifth Edition. CRC Press, 2023 https://routledge.pub/The-Care-of-the-Older-Person https://careoftheolderperson.com

134. Caplan, Ronald M: Lymph node: Glossary, The Care of the Older Person Fifth Edition. CRC Press, 2023 https://routledge.pub/The-Care-of-the-Older-Person https://careoftheolderperson.com

135. Morais, Jose: Aging: Introduction, The Care of the Older Person Fifth Edition. CRC Press, 2023 https://routledge.pub/The-Care-of-the-Older-Person https://careoftheolderperson.com

136. Ferrucci, Luigi: Reflections on Aging Research: Page 14, Nature Aging, Vol.1, January 2021 www.nature.com/nataging

137. Epigenetics http://epi.grants.cancer.gov/i/epigen-lg.jpg

138. Caplan, Ronald M: Epigenome: Glossary, The Care of the Older Person Fifth Edition. CRC Press, 2023 https://routledge.pub/The-Care-of-the-Older-Person https://careoftheolderperson.com

139. Caplan, Ronald M: Genome: Glossary, The Care of the Older Person Fifth Edition. CRC Press, 2023 https://routledge.pub/The-Care-of-the-Older-Person https://careoftheolderperson.com

140. Caplan, Ronald M: Zygote: Glossary, The Care of the Older Person Fifth Edition. CRC Press, 2023 https://routledge.pub/The-Care-of-the-Older-Person https://careoftheolderperson.com

141. Sirtuin genes https://www.ncbi.nlm.nih.gov/pubmed/18419308

142. Geroscience https://pubmed.ncbi.nlm.nih.gov/25417146/

143. Geroscience https://www.nia.nih.gov/research/dab/geroscience-intersectionbasic-aging-biology-chronic-disease-and-health

144. Geroprotector https://www.nature.com/articles/d41586-018-01668-0?utm_source=briefing-dy&utm_medium=email&utm_campaign=20180215WRONG https://www.nature.com/articles/d41586-018-01668-0?utm_source=briefing-dy&utm_medium=email&utm_campaign=20180215

145. Caplan, Ronald M: Senolytics: Glossary, The Care of the Older Person Fifth Edition. CRC Press, 2023 https://routledge.pub/The-Care-of-the-Older-Person https://careoftheolderperson.com

146. Neurodegenerative Disorders https://pubmed.ncbi.nlm.nih.gov/30258237/

147. Thinning of the Cerebral Cortex with Age https://www.frontiersin.org/articles/10.3389/fnagi.2017.00412/full 148. Gauthier, Serge: Update on Alzheimer's Disease, The Care of the Older Person Fifth Edition. CRC Press, 2023 https://routledge.pub/The-Care-of-the-Older-Person https://careoftheolderperson.com

149. Gauthier, Serge: Doctor, My Wife is Getting Forgetful, The Care of the Older Person Fifth Edition. CRC Press, 2023 https://routledge.pub/The-Care-of-the-OlderPerson https://careoftheolderperson.com

150. Caplan, Ronald M: Dementia: Glossary, The Care of the Older Person Fifth Edition. CRC Press, 2023 https://routledge.pub/The-Care-of-the-Older-Person https://careoftheolderperson.com

151. Caplan, Ronald M: Cognition: Glossary, The Care of the Older Person Fifth Edition. CRC Press, 2023 https://routledge.pub/The-Care-of-the-Older-Person https://careoftheolderperson.com

152. Caplan, Ronald M: Amyloid: Glossary, The Care of the Older Person Fifth Edition. CRC Press, 2023 https://routledge.pub/The-Care-of-the-Older-Person https://careoftheolderperson.com

153. Tau protein https://www.nia.nih.gov/health/what-happens-brain-alzheimers-disease

154. Caplan, Ronald M: Cognitive Impairment: Glossary, The Care of the Older Person Fifth Edition. CRC Press, 2023 https://routledge.pub/The-Care-of-the-Older-Person https://careoftheolderperson.com

155. Artificial Intelligence (AI) https://www.lexico.com/definition/artificial_intelligence

156. Caplan, Ronald M: Artificial Intelligence: Page Glossary, The Care of the Older Person Fifth Edition. CRC Press, 2023 https://routledge.pub/The-Care-of-the-OlderPerson https://careoftheolderperson.com

157. Machine Learning: https://www.ncbi.nlm.nih.gov/pmc/articles/PMC5831252/

158. Caplan, Ronald M: Machine Learning: Glossary, The Care of the Older Person Fifth Edition. CRC Press, 2023 https://routledge.pub/The-Care-of-the-Older-Person https://careoftheolderperson.com

159. Deep Learning https://arxiv.org/abs/1708.09843

160. Caplan, Ronald M: Deep Learning: Glossary, The Care of the Older Person Fifth Edition. CRC Press, 2023 https://routledge.pub/The-Care-of-the-Older-Person https://careoftheolderperson.com

161. Caplan, Ronald M: Neuromorphic Engineering: Glossary: The Care of the Older Person Fifth Edition. CRC Press, 2023 https://routledge.pub/The-Care-of-the-OlderPerson https://careoftheolderperson.com

162. Concussion https://www.cdc.gov/headsup/basics/concussion_whatis.html

163. Traumatic Brain Injury https://www.cdc.gov/traumaticbraininjury/severe.html

164. Near Death Experience https://www.frontiersin.org/articles/10.3389/fpsyg.2018.01424/full

165. Cardiac Tamponade Revisited: Texas Heart Institute https://www.ncbi.nlm.nih.gov/pmc/articles/PMC1995065/#:~:text=Jugular%20venous%20distention%2C%20if%20not,volume%20to%20increase%20and%20equilibrate

166. Pulsus Paradoxus in Cardiac Tamponade https://pubmed.ncbi.nlm.nih.gov/10150624/

167. Pulsus Paradoxus https://www.ncbi.nlm.nih.gov/books/NBK482292/

168. Caplan, Ronald M: Transient Ischemic Arteriospasm: Glossary. The Care of the Older Person Fifth Edition. CRC Press, 2023 https://routledge.pub/The-Care-of-theOlder-Person https://careoftheolderperson.com

169. M-Theory https://www.space.com/string-theory-11-dimensions-universe.html

170. Walt Whitman and Maurice Bucke https://whitmanarchive.org/biography/correspondence/tei/med.00705.html

171. Fail Safe Mechanism https://www.ncbi.nlm.nih.gov/pmc/articles/PMC4175050/

172. Fail Safe Mechanism https://elifesciences.org/articles/20069

173. Aducanumab 174. https://www.ncbi.nlm.nih.gov/books/NBK573062/

174. Lecanemab-irmb. https://www.ncbi.nlm.nih.gov/pmc/articles/PMC9768996/

175. Assembly Theory. https://www.nature.com/articles/s41467-021-23258-x

176. Superposition https://scienceexchange.caltech.edu/topics/quantum-scienceexplained/quantum-superposition

177. Quantum states https://www.nature.com/articles/d41586-023-00968-4?WT.ec_id=NATURE-20230413&utm_source=nature_etoc&utm_medium=email&utm_campaign=20230413&sap-outbound-id=74BFCB67E887AB195D075B5234FA4EA5F7D4055F

178. On the Origin of Time: Stephen Hawking's Final Theory Thomas Hertog Torva/Bantam (2023),

179. Review: Robert P. Crease https://www.nature.com/articles/d41586023-00977-3?utm_source=Nature+Briefing&utm_campaign=f1fe2b3b43briefing-dy-20230414&utm_medium=email&utm_term=0_c9dfd39373f1fe2b3b43-42544483

180. Fifth dimension https://sciencing.com/5th-dimension-11369444.html

181. Fourth dimension: Space-Time https://bigthink.com/technology innovation/hints-of-the-4th-dimension-have-been-detected-by-physicists/

182. Koan https://bigthink.com/neuropsych/what-is-a-koan/

183. General Relativity (Einstein) https://bigthink.com/starts-with-abang/einstein-general-theory-relativity-equation/

184. Superposition https://www.sciencenews.org/article/sapphire-schrodingers-catquantum?utm_source=Nature+Briefing&utm_campaign=8b15a3be52-briefing-dy20230427&utm_medium=email&utm_term=0_c9dfd39373-8b15a3be52-42544483

185. Barberi, T., et al. Nat Biotechnol, 21, 1200-1207 (2003)

186. Tabar, V, et al. Nat. Med.doi: 10.1038/NM 1732 (2008)

187. Caplan, Ronald M: Nuclease: Glossary: The Care of the Older Person: Fifth Edition. CRC Press 2023 https://routledge.pub/The-Care-of-the-Older-Person https://careoftheolderperson.com

188. Brain activity near death doi: 10.1126/science.adi5224

189. Lightman, Alan: The Transcendent Brain: Pantheon, Random House 2023

190. Mendelssohn, Moses: Phaedon: Immortality of the Soul, The Death of Socrates: 1767. https://archive.schillerinstitute.com/transl/mend_phadn_cullen.html

191. Plato: Phaedo https://www.sparknotes.com/philosophy/phaedo/summary/

192. Immanuel Kant KpV 5:122

193. Metaphysics https://www.thebritishacademy.ac.uk/blog/what-is-metaphysics/

194. Immanuel Kant and metaphysics https://plato.stanford.edu/entries/kantmetaphysics/

195. Immanuel Kant and metaphysics https://plato.stanford.edu/entries/kant/#:~:text=From%20this%20Kant%20conclu des%20that,necessarily%20conforms%20to%20certain%20laws.

196. Artificial Intelligence and medicine Hie, B. L. et al. Nature Biotechnol. https://doi.org/10.1038/s41587-023-01763-2 (2023)

197. Senolytics Zhang L, Pitcher LE, Yousefzadeh MJ, Niedernhofer LJ, Robbins PD, Zhu Y. Cellular senescence: a key therapeutic target in aging and diseases. Journal of Clinical Investigation. 2022; 132(15):e158450.

198. Chalmers, David (1995). "Facing up to the problem of consciousness". Journal of Consciousness Studies. **2** (3): 200–219

199. López-Rubio, E. Computational Functionalism for the Deep Learning Era. Minds & Machines **28**, 667–688 (2018). https://doi.org/10.1007/s11023-018-9480-7

200. Riess, Adam https://www.britannica.com/science/dark-matter

201. https://www.forbes.com/sites/startswithabang/2021/08/24/who-really-discovered-dark-matter-fritz-zwicky-or-vera-rubin/?sh=5dccf15217a7

202. IIT https://doi.org/10.1101/2023.06.23.546249

203. IIT https://www.nature.com/articles/d41586-023-02971-1?utm_source=Nature+Briefing&utm_campaign=84936ca310-briefing-dy-20230921&utm_medium=email&utm_term=0_c9dfd39373-84936ca310-42544483

204. GNW https://pubmed.ncbi.nlm.nih.gov/32135090/

205. Hard Problem; Recurrent processing Theory, Higher-Order Thought Theory https://plato.stanford.edu/entries/consciousness-neuroscience/

206. IIT https://www.nature.com/articles/nrn.2016.44/

207. IIT https://iep.utm.edu/integrated-information-theory-of-consciousness/

208. Brain Cells https://www.nature.com/articles/d41586-023-03192-2?utm_source=Live+Audience&utm_campaign=e89a56e438-briefing-dy-20231013&utm_medium=email&utm_term=0_b27a691814-e89a56e438-49155223

209. Three-dimensional robotic surgery https://pubmed.ncbi.nlm.nih.gov/35015896/

210. Carl Sagan https://www.nature.com/articles/d41586-023-03240-x?WT.ec_id=NATURE-20231019&utm_source=nature_etoc&utm_medium=email&utm_campaign=20231019&sap-outbound-id=5F1440F59679AC88C039B4E0BB1E0E8A3916AA29

211. DNA Repair https://www.nature.com/articles/d42473-023-00138-0?sap-outbound-id=609DEC7CF700115BB928163AAC1CDA5987F6DF36

212. ADLS https://www.ncbi.nlm.nih.gov/books/NBK470404/

213. IADL https://www.ncbi.nlm.nih.gov/books/NBK553126/

214. CRISPR-Cas9 https://www.nature.com/articles/d41586-023-03697-w?utm_source=Live+Audience&utm_campaign=2ccfe95815-briefing-dy-20231124&utm_medium=email&utm_term=0_b27a691814-2ccfe95815-49155223

215. Oppenheim, Jonathan: Postquantum Theory of Classical Gravity? https://journals.aps.org/prx/abstract/10.1103/PhysRevX.13.041040

216. Qubit. https://www.quantum-inspire.com/kbase/what-is-a-qubit

217. Superposition https://www.researchgate.net/publication/258566887_The_Superposition_Principle_in_Quantum_Mechanics_did_the_rockenter_the_foundation_surreptitiously

218. https://www.science.org/doi/10.1126/science.adf8999

219. Entanglement https://www.sciencedaily.com/terms/quantum_entanglement.htm

220. Sickle Cell Disease https://www.fda.gov/news-events/press-announcements/fda-approves-first-gene-therapies-treat-patients-sickle-cell-disease

221. Front. Immunol., 30 November 2023
Sec. Cytokines and Soluble Mediators in Immunity
Volume 14 - 2023 https://doi.org/10.3389/fimmu.2023.1286380
A predictive model for disease severity based on IgG subtypes and machine learning among COVID-19 elderly patients

222. MACHINE LEARNING
https://www.ncbi.nlm.nih.gov/pmc/articles/PMC5831252/
https://www.sciencedirect.com/science/article/pii/S093336571730009X
https://www.techemergence.com/machine-learning-in-pharma-medicine/
https://www.healthcareitnews.com/projects/ai-and-machinelearning?mkt_tok=eyJpIjoiWVRJNE5qTmpPRE01WmpabSIsInQiOiJCcktaVzljSVRpVVpWQ3FYa2lEazc1WHlQSGc5bUV3YXlwTFVtbEdvM2RjSVY

223. Chen, E.K Does Quantum Theory imply the entire Universe is preordained? Nature **624**, 513-515 (2023) doi: https://doi.org/10.1038/d41586-023-04024-z

224. Determinism https://www.britannica.com/topic/determinism

225. Epigenetic reprogramming https://www.nature.com/articles/s43587-023-00539-2

226. Yamanaka, S.; Blau, H.M. Nuclear reprogramming to a pluripotent state by three approaches https://pubmed.ncbi.nlm.nih.gov/20535199/

227. Susskind, Leonard: arXiv:1708.03040 [**hep-th**]

228. Entin, Martin: Practical Surgery of the Hand. Saunders Orthopedic Clinics of North America 1973

229. https://plato.stanford.edu/entries/heraclitus/#UniOpp

230. Zee, Anthony: Quantum Field Theory in a Nutshell https://books.google.com/books?hl=en&lr=&id=XrumDwAAQBAJ&oi=fnd&pg=PR15&dq=quantum+field+theory+explained&ots=w5pxLYNCco&sig=nRJ0pknskYOI3dXElx8N9O81Nls#v=onepage&q=quantum%20field%20theory%20explained&f=false

231. Meier,C.A, Ed: Atom and archetype: The Pauli-Jung Letters 1932-1958 https://catdir.loc.gov/catdir/samples/prin031/2001016323.pdf

232. https://www.kingjamesbibleonline.org/ Hebrews 4:16; Exodus 33, 12-13; Psalm 84:11

233. Special Relativity: Albert Einstein https://www.space.com/36273-theory-special-relativity.html

234. General Relativity: Albert Einstein: https://www.britannica.com/science/general-relativity

235. Terminal lucidity Nahm https://pubmed.ncbi.nlm.nih.gov/21764150/

236. Paradoxical lucidity https://www.ncbi.nlm.nih.gov/pmc/articles/PMC9924090/

ABOUT THE AUTHOR

RONALD M. CAPLAN MDCM, FACS, FACOG, FRCSC is an Obstetrician Gynecologist, medical author and editor who has spent his professional life studying and treating the medical conditions that impact humanity, and their relation to the dynamic society in which we all live.

Dr. Caplan's work goes back almost sixty years to the World's Fair EXPO67 Meditheatre, Miracles in Modern Medicine, where the opening sequence of his delivery of a healthy Rh Positive baby by an Rh Negative mother, an event never seen before by a large lay audience, was viewed by 2.5 million people.

In that same general timeframe, he accomplished the world's first delivery of a baby from a mother with a deceased donor kidney transplant.

Dr. Caplan has been a Faculty Member at two major Universities: Joan and Sanford I. Weill Medical College of Cornell University in New York City, where he was an early proponent and practitioner of minimally invasive surgery, and McGill University in Montreal, Canada. He has been appointed Clinical

Associate Professor Emeritus of Obstetrics and Gynecology at The Joan and Sanford I. Weill Medical College of Cornell University.

Dr. Caplan is a Fellow of the American College of Obstetrics and Gynecology, a Fellow of the American College of Surgeons, and a Fellow of the Royal College of Surgeons (Canada).

Dr. Caplan is the editor of three medical textbooks, *The Care of the Older Person* (CRC Press, Routledge, Taylor & Francis Group, 2022) which is now in its Fifth Edition, with a Chinese Edition and an audiobook; *Principles of Obstetrics* (Williams & Wilkins, 1982), including Portuguese and Spanish editions; and *Advances in Obstetrics and Gynecology* (Williams & Wilkins, 1978), including a Spanish edition. He has written trade and mass-market books, including most recently *Long Life Strategy* (Springer, 2024), now in its Second Edition and a German edition; *Your Pregnancy* (with Betty Rothbart: Quill William Morrow, 1992), *The Doctor's Guide to Pregnancy after Thirty* (Ivy Books, Ballantine 1987; Macmillan 1986), and *Pregnant is Beautiful* (Pocket Books, Simon & Schuster, 1985; Appleton, 1981).

Dr. Caplan is Managing Member of RMC Publishing LLC, https://rmcpublishingllc.com.